WHAT GOD HATH WROUGHT

WHAT GOD HATH WROUGHT

Eastern's First Thirty-five Years

Edited by

Gilbert L. Guffin, *President*

The Eastern Baptist Theological Seminary

THE JUDSON PRESS

CHICAGO / PHILADELPHIA / LOS ANGELES

WHAT GOD HATH WROUGHT

Library of Congress Catalog Card No. 60-9653

PRINTED IN THE UNITED STATES OF AMERICA

FOREWORD

"HISTORY," SAID GIBBON, "is indeed little more than the register of the crimes, foibles, and misfortunes of mankind."

Not all history is such, as is fully attested by the witness of the Church through nearly 2000 years. To be sure, that witness occasionally has been mixed with "foibles" . . . if not with "misfortunes," and sometimes has had its low tides. But more often it has risen to notable crests and has swept incalculable blessings in toward the shores of human need.

The history of Eastern is certainly not a record of foibles and misfortunes, to say nothing of crimes. Naturally, this history has been marked at times with the human weaknesses of those of us who have taken part in it; but except for this, it is the record of extensive, remarkable achievement. Humbly and with thanksgiving for the privilege of participation, those of us who have been identified in one way or another with The Eastern Baptist Theological Seminary during the past thirty-five years would beg all who read this story to give audience to us as we declare only what we believe to be the "miracles and wonders which God hath wrought." It is His work and we have been but His servants. We are profoundly and abidingly grateful to Him that He has been pleased to give fruit to our labors.

It seems appropriate at this point not only to record our abiding gratitude to God for the record made possible in the life of this Seminary, but also for me personally to state my deep indebtedness to my honored predecessors into whose labors I have been privileged to enter and the fruit of whose sowing I have been allowed to reap. It was not my good fortune to know Eastern's first president, Dr. Ball, but the story of his ministry, North and South, was evidently a notable one. In the Southern Baptist Encyclopedia the following is recorded about him: "Pastor, teacher, youth leader . . . dean of the Bible Department at Hardin-Simmons College . . . professor of Comparative Religion and Missions in Southwestern Baptist Theological Seminary . . . founder of the Baptist Student Missionary Movement . . . forerunner of the Baptist Student Union . . . executive secretary of the American Baptist Student Union . . . pastor of the Wissinoming Baptist Church, Philadelphia. . . ."

All of the above, Dr. Ball did before he became the first president of Eastern. Dr. Ball obviously was a pioneer, a man possessed with creative imagination and a soul of great dedication. He was not provincial, but was at home anywhere, especially among Baptists.

Although I did not know Dr. Ball, I have had the joy and benediction of knowing both President de Blois and President Palmer. I shall never forget the inspiration and profit of studying personally under the former nor the moving experience of receiving my doctor's degree at the hand of the latter. Through the past ten years of my service at Eastern, Dr. Palmer has been a source of constant encouragement and has often shared his good council and wisdom with me. Surely no former president was ever more careful to avoid restricting the freedom of his successor or trying to dictate to the one who followed him. I freely acknowledge that the progress which has been possible over these years of my service has been in great measure the result of the wise leadership and constructive ministry of Dr. Palmer and of those who preceded him.

Often have I been reminded as I have thought of the service of my predecessors that "others laid the foundation. . . ." How well they laid it, subsequent chapters will attempt, at least briefly, to relate.

To the trustees, both laymen and ministers, many of whom have been possessed of remarkable abilities and all of whom have contributed inestimably to the development of the school; to the faculty, dedicated and able as they have been and are; to all the devoted and faithful staff and administrative personnel; and to all the others who have been participants in the building and on-going of Eastern Seminary, deepest appreciation is hereby warmly and readily given.

Finally, especial thanks are due the committee which has worked with me in the preparation of the manuscript for this book. Dean Carl H. Morgan, my distinguished co-worker, in addition to preparing the chapter which bears his name, has lent valuable assistance in helping to edit the entire volume. Dr. Norman H. Maring, our able registrar and professor of Church History, also has given many constructive suggestions, in addition to preparing his informative chapter. Dr. Gordon H. Baker (to whom a more extended tribute is paid at the conclusion of Chapter III) has given months of time to the reviewing of the minutes of the board, as well as other historical data gathered since the founding of the school. Though Dr. Baker personally had a significant part in helping to make the record which has been put down in these source materials, it was quite an exacting chore for him thus to retrace the developments of the school. For this devoted service, as well as for the years of loyal and dedicated usefulness he has poured into the work of Eastern since the day he took part in the first meeting which led to the founding of the school, an adequate expression of appreciation would be difficult to frame. To Dr. Benjamin P. Browne, trustee of the Seminary and executive director of the Division of Christian Publications of the Board of Education and Publication of the American Baptist Convention, and to Dr. Arthur B. Crabtree, professor of Theology, for their valuable contributions; to my assistant, Mr. John A. Baird, Jr., and to Mr. Thomas P. Ferguson of our Public Relations office, for their handling of all the technical details connected with the publication of this volume; and to my faithful secretary, Miss Esther George; to the dean's secretary, Miss Jeanne LeRoy; to the faculty secretary, Miss Maxine Benson; and to the assistant registrar, Miss Phyllis Anderson, heartiest appreciation is also given for their help with the typing.

Finally, to the board of trustees for its willingness to authorize the publication of this history of Eastern's past thirty-five years, warm gratitude is again expressed. It is hoped that the trustees will have cause to believe this authorization was advisedly given.

—Gilbert L. Guffin

Philadelphia, Pa.
April 15, 1960

CONTENTS

INTRODUCTION

by

BENJAMIN P. BROWNE

WHO CAN MEASURE INFLUENCE? Yet is anything in our human life more powerful? Science has devised no instruments for the exact measurement of this subtle but pervasive force in both individual and institutional life. Least of all are we able to measure specifically the influence which is spiritual. Indeed, the Spirit is like the wind, which "bloweth where it listeth." We may see and hear its results, but we cannot tell whence it comes nor where it goes. But so real and penetrating is the influence of dedicated Christian personality that in the days of the early church the sick and the lame were brought into the narrow streets that the shadow of Peter might fall upon them as he passed by. Not only every Christian person but also every Christian institution possesses an unconscious but effective influence wherever its shadow falls.

Therefore, an account of the influence of a Christian theological seminary must always fall short of the full record of its achievement. The complete record can be fully known only in heaven, while much of it must lie unwritten in a thousand human hearts and homes, known only to God.

Furthermore, any evaluation of an institution solely in terms of bricks and mortar, campus and budget, statistics and enrollment, can be utterly inadequate. Much more than these, an institution is the influence of its dedicated and scholarly faculty, together with the quality and serious-mindedness of its students, and possibly also of a host of other persons who are touched by them.

Remembering that seminaries exist to train undershepherds of Christ's flock, Eastern has poured hundreds of men into the pastoral ministry. This must always be a primary task and glory of a Baptist theological seminary.

Nor has the sending of missionaries to lands abroad been neglected. Eastern has sent scores of well-trained missionaries into both home and foreign fields. Her evangelists in pulpits, in schools, in hospitals, in the armed forces, and in mission stations have summoned countless souls to the joy of salvation through the redeeming grace of our Lord Jesus Christ.

True it is that though the vast majority of its graduates serve within the co-operative fellowship of the American Baptist Convention, some of its graduates also contribute their talents and leadership to several other conventions and denominations. This may be said to be the ecumenical outreach of Eastern, though strangely enough, this has sometimes been a cause of criticism on the part of those who claim to possess the ecumenical fervor. Eastern remains essentially an American Baptist school, but it has never refused to train ministers for evangelical service in any fellowship.

The influence of Eastern's faculty extends to its sharing of its members with a number of other widely-known Baptist theological seminaries, some of which have several Eastern people on their staffs. Older seminaries have turned to Eastern for personnel to strengthen their faculties. In the college field also, Eastern has provided presidents, deans, department heads, professors, and instructors.

Quite remarkable also, as statistics will show, has been the contribution which Eastern has made to the executive and managerial work of various divisions and departments of the organized services of the American Baptist Convention.

After a survey of the far-reaching influence of Eastern through its distinguished faculty and its more than 1,500 alumni, one stands amazed at the realization that all of this has been achieved by a very young seminary. Eastern is only thirty-five years old. Beside older seminaries which reckon a hundred years and more of activity, Eastern seems to have had a precocious growth. Though it has served less than a third of the time of some seminaries, its contribution seems to be no whit behind those of its older sister institutions.

Bearing in mind that spiritual influence is not really measurable, statistics sometimes help to give a general, though partial, picture. Some of these statistics will appear in the chapters that follow.

The Seminary has several hundred of its graduates serving as pastors in American Baptist churches. Many of them are pastors of very strong churches which have made outstanding records of growth, as well as of financial contributions to the American Baptist Convention. In those areas where the denomination appears to be having its most exciting growth, for example in Southern California, Eastern men are giving pastoral leadership in a large majority of the churches.

Eastern's contribution to the life and activity of the American Baptist Convention was strikingly revealed in a recent report of the Conference on the Ministry of the Convention. This report indicated that in a survey of the background and training of the pastors of the American Baptist Convention, Eastern, despite the brevity of its history, now has the second largest number of alumni of any seminary serving churches of the Convention. The one seminary having a larger number was founded more than a hundred years earlier.

In addition to this contribution to the pastoral field of several denominations, Eastern has also a good group of chaplains serving in the armed forces and an impressive number of directors of Christian education. Relative to its brief span of service, Eastern undoubtedly has taken a lead position among our seminaries in terms of providing fully trained directors of Christian education.

In a similar way, Eastern has sought to train men with a concern for the mission of Christ to all the world, and its missionaries have gone out to serve in several different mission fields in some thirty different countries. Its greatest number of missionaries, however, serve now under the American Baptist Home and Foreign Mission Boards.

In recounting the contribution of The Eastern Baptist Theological Seminary to American life, one must not overlook the significance of Eastern Baptist College which once operated as a collegiate division of the Seminary, but now stands on its own feet as a four-year accredited college. Since 1932 there have been, at this writing, 517 graduates of the college (about half of these since 1952), and these graduates are giving their Christian witness in American life as ministers, college presidents, faculty members, schoolteachers, businessmen, doctors, lawyers, and church leaders.

The prospects of Eastern's future contributions are bright. With accreditation on a high rating achieved some years ago, the Seminary and the College both show themselves to be strong and growing institutions with a positive evangelical witness. They are pouring increasing numbers of trained, intelligent, dedicated leaders into the religious life of America, and indeed, of the world.

I

CONSERVATIVE BUT PROGRESSIVE

by

NORMAN H. MARING

"We have enough theological seminaries!" exclaimed a man, upon hearing of the founding of The Eastern Baptist Theological Seminary. With eight seminaries and two missionary training schools, the Northern Baptist Convention did seem well supplied with institutions to prepare ministers. Moreover, the existing seminaries were complaining of a shortage of students. It is not surprising, therefore, that some people questioned the need for another seminary.

However, judging by the enthusiastic response to Eastern's early appeal for support, there was a place for another theological school. Financial contributions from churches and individuals, as well as the number of students enrolled in the first year, furnished evidence of a widespread sense of need for a conservative seminary. Although some charged that Eastern was formed to promote an ultra-conservative ministry, the founding trustees were not extremists. They believed that there was room for a seminary which would represent a sane and healthy conservatism. In establishing Eastern, they thought that they were fulfilling a need long felt by "many leaders of our denomination who are loyal to historic Baptist ideals and interpretation of the Scriptures." [1]

Not all of the reactions to the launching of Eastern in 1925 were favorable. On the part of some people there was open hostility. The correspondent of one periodical sneered: "A group of Baptists, announcing themselves 'God's loyal people,' met in Philadelphia recently and adopted a 'five-point' creed with a high church statement." [2] Sarcastic in tone, this news article revealed a lack of understanding of the new seminary's purpose and spirit.

Another part of the denomination, more moderate in its disapproval, was represented by Dr. Arthur C. Baldwin, Philadelphia pastor and denominational leader. Informing his readers about the seminary, he explained: "Beyond doubt it expresses the dissatisfaction of Eastern fundamentalists with our seminaries and their courses." His attitude is reflected in the following words:

> "I think it is evident that the new school is inevitable. The names of its officers assure this. They are conscientious, responsible men and have the ability to push through what they undertake. It is needless to add, I suppose, that many of us here deeply regret the undertaking. We feel that it is divisive, unnecessary, and will divert funds which ought to be used to strengthen present denominational work." [3]

The surmise of Dr. Baldwin that Eastern was the offspring of the "fundamentalists" was correct, for the new seminary was a direct outgrowth of the fundamentalist movement in the Northern Baptist Convention. Such a statement of origins may easily be misunderstood, however, since it is almost impossible today to obtain a fair picture of that movement in its early days. There is little resemblance between the original Northern Baptist "fundamentalists" and the stereotype of fundamentalism which now prevails. In part the confusion regarding this term stems from the work of unsympathetic historians; in part it is due to the fact that extremists gradually took over the movement. Within the theological conservatism of the 1920's there were many shades of opinion and attitude; it was a much more complex and variegated movement than historians often have recognized.

The most recent history of fundamentalism [4] conveys the impression that its leaders were ignorant obscurantists who opposed new ideas in general. Accordingly, their interests are narrowly interpreted, and the author sums them up under "the five points of fundamentalism": infallibility of the Scriptures, the Virgin Birth, the substitutionary atonement, the resurrection of Jesus Christ, and the premillennial return of Christ. Under the caption, "Characteristics of Fundamentalism," he lists violence in thought and language, ignorance and illiteracy, anti-intellectualism, and egotism. Confusion regarding this term is increased by the fact that today fundamentalism has largely been repudiated by those who once marched under its banner. Dr. Harold Ockenga, for example, has declared that fundamentalism has failed,[5] and Dr. Edward J. Carnell is devastating in his criticism of the movement.[6]

In view of the image of fundamentalism which is current in the public mind, an assertion of a fundamentalist origin of Eastern Seminary will almost certainly be misleading, for fundamentalism originally stood for a moderate conservatism, championed with a temperate spirit, and carried on within the brotherhood of the Northern Baptist Convention. It was not separatistic, belligerent, anti-evolutionist, negative about social reform, or any of many other things which are commonly ascribed to fundamentalism. Therefore, it is necessary to reconstruct the beginnings of the fundamentalists in order to interpret the statement that Eastern was the offspring of fundamentalists.

The controversy between modernism and fundamentalism arose after 1918, but the storm had long been brewing. Confronted by many challenges in the nineteenth century, the American churches had felt their traditional practice and thought threatened at many points. The industrial growth of the country raised problems which troubled the conscience of the Church, while Darwinism, sociological and psychological theory, the study of comparative religions, and the so-called "Higher Criticism" of the Bible tested inherited theological systems. Along with others, the Baptists were deeply involved in the new currents.

Most crucial of all the problems faced by Baptists was that which centered around the Bible. Like other Protestants, they had held the Scriptures of the Old and New Testaments as authoritative, but had not examined very critically the nature of that authority. Many assumed that an authoritative Bible must be an inerrant one, although Baptist theologians of unquestioned orthodoxy had often refused to commit themselves to static theories of inspiration. As Biblical scholarship became more critical, and as historical and literary criticism was applied to the Scriptures, many seminary professors became convinced that claims of inerrancy were untenable. During the fifty years preceding World War I, the Baptist seminaries of the North went through the throes of wrestling with perplexing Biblical questions. By 1918 the rights of a reverent criticism were generally acknowledged, and a number of conclusions had been commonly accepted in the theological schools.

The acceptance of such conclusions as the composite authorship of the Pentateuch, the late dating of the Psalms, and the existence of historical discrepancies, however, did not necessarily lead to one's becoming a theological liberal. Most of the professors in the Baptist seminaries were warmly evangelical, and although they conceded the legitimacy of Biblical criticism, they were generally opposed to the negative emphases of "destructive criticism." At the same time, changed views of the Bible led to corresponding changes in theology. Abandonment of an appeal to an infallible Bible necessitated the substitution of some other definition of the authority on which Christian faith rested. Some men took their stand upon "eternal truths" taught in the Bible, while others stressed Christian "experience" as the test of truth. The tendency was to move toward a one-sided appeal to the subjective elements in Christianity, rather than toward an objective authority. Eventually, a liberal theology developed in which there was a minimizing of sin, an excessive optimism about human history, and a decreasing sense of the need for redemption and of the significance of the person and work of Jesus Christ. Theology veered away from supernaturalism toward an over-emphasis upon the immanence of God in natural processes, and in many cases Biblical studies were devoted to the process of tearing down old ideas with little attempt to give the student anything to put in the place of his shattered views. The acids of modernity were dissolving the faith of young ministers, and the faith was beginning to suffer from the paralysis of analysis.

A protest against theological change was slow to develop. Tensions were apparent in the 1890's, but the issues were not yet clear and the leaders necessary to crystallize dissenting opinions had not yet appeared. As early as 1897, one Baptist leader had noted that "the lines are being drawn, and the party spirit is gaining strength." With prophetic insight, he warned: "If the old and the new are to fight, it will be a fight all along the line, among pastors, between schools, in churches, associations, conventions, national societies." [7]

Although there were earlier movements opposing the current trends in Biblical and theological studies, the conflicts did not come to a head in the Northern Baptist Convention until after 1918. A few Baptists had participated in interdenominational groups which had held prophetic conferences, stressed premillennial programs, and also attacked the theological schools which showed signs of shifting away from orthodoxy. A series of twelve booklets called *The Fundamentals* was published between 1909 and 1915 under the auspices of the wealthy Stewart brothers, who also founded the Bible Institute of Los Angeles. Dr. A. C. Dixon, editor of the first five of these volumes, was a Baptist, but he was by then becoming more interested in interdenominational work than in the Convention; hardly any other Baptists contributed to the volumes. Among the contributors to the series were quite a few respectable scholars. The addresses and articles represented a serious effort to deal with basic issues, and were not much given to premillennialism or other peripheral questions. However, there was as yet no party which was actually called "the fundamentalists," nor was the word "fundamentalism" in use. There were frequent references in those days to "fundamentals," but the designation "fundamentalist" had not yet been coined.

Following World War I, a protest movement against liberal theology developed in the Northern Baptist Convention. A decline in seminary enrollments helped to focus attention upon the theological schools and the colleges. Although the war itself accounted for a decrease in the number of ministerial students, many people blamed the shortage of recruits for the ministry upon the seminaries. In 1918, Dr.

Cortland Myers wrote an article on this subject and charged that "this abominable new theology imported from Germany is one of the principal causes of the trouble." [8] All of the Baptist seminaries were invited to state their convictions in the pages of *The Watchman-Examiner,* and three of them did so while others explained the difficulty of complying with the request. Suspicion toward the seminaries was indicative of a rising tide of dissatisfaction with the state of theology in the schools.

Misgivings about the theological institutions were heightened in 1918 by a statement of Dr. Augustus H. Strong. In a book on missions, he asserted: "The theological seminaries of almost all our denominations are becoming so infected with this grievous error that they are not so much organs of Christ as they are organs of Antichrist. . . . We are losing our faith in the Bible and our determination to stand for its teachings." [9] Since he had been president of one of the seminaries, his words carried a special weight of authority and increased apprehensions about the orthodoxy of the seminaries.

It is against this background of alarm over the spread of modernism that the emergence of the fundamentalists must be seen. What has not always been recognized is that there is more than one type of dissent among the conservatives. There was general agreement among them that there are certain essential elements, or "fundamentals," of the gospel which do not change, and that these center around the person and work of Jesus Christ. With regard to particular interpretations and to the nature and extent of their objections, as well as to attitudes and methods, there were significant differences within conservatism which ought to be clearly noted. Those who led in the fundamentalist movement of the Northern Baptist Convention were moderates both in theological position and temperament.

The origin of the fundamentalists as a self-conscious group is to be found in a conference on "The Fundamentals of Our Baptist Faith" held in Buffalo in 1920. Called to meet just prior to the sessions of the Northern Baptist Convention, the invitation was addressed to all Baptists within the bounds of the denomination. It stated:

> "We view with increasing alarm the havoc which rationalism is working in our churches as evidenced by the drift upon the part of many of our ministers from the fundamentals of our holy faith. . . .
>
> "We believe that there rests upon us as Baptists an immediate and urgent duty to restate, reaffirm, and re-emphasize the fundamentals of our New Testament faith. Beyond all doubt the vast majority of our Baptist people are as loyal as were our fathers to our Baptist principles . . . , but this loyalty will not long continue unless something is done to stay the rising tide of liberalism and rationalism." [10]

Among the one hundred or more names appended to the invitation were men of varied shades of conservative opinion. Some extremists were included, but they would eventually withdraw from this movement, holding that it was too timid and unaggressive. Several of the persons whose names were appended were moderates; they continued to be active in this movement, and were to become trustees and teachers at Eastern. A glance at the program for the conference shows that there was little of a sensational character. The only two of the eleven addresses which contained controversial notes were those by Dr. A. C. Dixon and Dr. W. B. Riley. Neither of these men was representative of the movement as a whole, nor played an important part in shaping its future. The days of the aging Dixon were numbered, and Dr. Riley was too impetuous to work with the moderates who controlled the fundamentalists.

It was shortly after the Convention of 1920 that Dr. Curtis Lee Laws proposed that the term "Fundamentalist" be adopted to designate those who had met at Buffalo, and who wished to work for the preservation of the fundamentals of the faith. "We here and now move," he wrote, "that a new word be adopted to describe the men among us who insist that the landmarks shall not be removed. . . . We suggest that those who still cling to the great fundamentals and who mean to do battle royal for the fundamentals shall be called 'Fundamentalists.'" [11]

Thus, it was in connection with a particular party within the Convention that "Fundamentalist" was first used, and for several years the name was applied primarily with reference to this particular entity. These Fundamentalists were not affiliated with the World's Christian Fundamentals Association, nor with any other interdenominational organization. They are to be distinguished also from the Baptist Bible Union, which was formed in 1923 by Drs. T. T. Shields, W. B. Riley, J. Frank Norris, and others who believed the Fundamentalists to be too tame and slow-moving.

A comparison of the Fundamentalists with the Baptist Bible Union will help to clarify the position of the former. Although the two groups stood for the defense of the fundamentals of the faith, they differed in their origins, constituencies, spirit, methods, and interests.

The Bible Union, organized in 1923, received its initial impetus from a similar body in England, and the invitation to the organizing meeting was signed by three officers of the English Bible Union. The Fundamentalists, on the other hand, was a spontaneous movement among the Northern Baptists and continued to work within the denomination, whereas the other group worked among all Baptists in North America. "Fundamentalists," wrote Dr. Frank Goodchild, pastor of Central Baptist Church in New York City and leader of the Fundamentalists from their beginning, "have felt that the purpose for which they came into being was a sort of family matter, and could be attended to best by members of the family." [12]

With regard to spirit and method, the Bible Union was the more militant of the two, and it sometimes charged that the Fundamentalists were traitors to the cause. "The diagnosis of the Bible Unioner as militant," asserted Goodchild, "is entirely correct. Perhaps belligerent would be the better word. . . . The Fundamentalists . . . have for the most part not cried out in resentment and have refused to vituperate." The Bible Unionists talked of secession from the Convention, and they encouraged church members to withdraw support from Convention causes to support faith missions. The Fundamentalists as a whole urged co-operation in the Convention programs even where there might have seemed to be reason for disagreement over policies. "Fundamentalists have had no thought of secession," declared Dr. Goodchild in 1925, thus reiterating a sentiment more than once stated in the editorials of *The Watchman-Examiner.*

Differences on particular issues also separated these two conservative parties. The Bible Unioners were vigorous crusaders against evolutionist views, but the Fundamentalists made no issue of this. During the months of the Scopes trial in Tennessee, Dr. Laws made little mention of the case in *The Watchman-Examiner.* Indeed, he was not greatly disturbed over the issue. "Whether the teaching of evolution in the schools is warranted," he wrote, "depends on how it is taught." [13] His only concern in the matter was that evolutionary theory should be theistic.

Another matter of importance to the Bible Union was premillennialism. Its doctrinal statement required belief in this doctrine. On the other hand, the Fundamentalist movement in the Convention was "in no sense a premillennialist movement," [14] explained Dr. Laws. Since people kept charging the Fundamentalists with promoting premillennialism, Laws had more than once to reiterate the denial that there was any identity between this movement and that subject. "We are not particularly interested in pre-millenarianism nor in post-millenarianism," he said. Fundamentalists were satisfied with a belief in the actual return of Christ, but took no stand on questions about the millennium.

What, then, did the Fundamentalists stand for? The answer was simple and obvious to Dr. Laws, Dr. Goodchild, and others. They were at a loss to understand why there were such persistent misconceptions about their movement. They took their stand upon what had been considered as Baptist orthodoxy all along. They advocated no new ideas; it was the Modernists who were the innovators. "When will sensible people realize that the Fundamentalists are standing simply for the faith that all men everywhere adopted before the advent of modernism?" asked Dr. Laws. He continued: "Fundamentalism, pure and simple, is merely a defense of what practically all Christians believed twenty-five years ago." [15] The same refrain is found in the words of Dr. Goodchild: "Fundamentalists stand where loyal Baptists have always stood." Annoyed with being tagged with the "five points" libel, Dr. Goodchild declared that the five points of the Fundamentalists actually were these: "We believe that the Bible is God's Word. . . . Fundamentalists believe just as strongly in the church as in the Bible. . . . Fundamentalists believe in the denomination. . . . Fundamentalists believe in schools. . . . Fundamentalists believe thoroughly in missions."[16]

The case of the Fundamentalists was a reasonable one. They stood essentially where Baptists had stood a generation before, and it was the new generation which was asking for new definitions and interpretations. Nor did these Fundamentalists oppose progress and change; they were willing to tolerate many points of disagreement. They did not object to Biblical criticism so long as it was carried on in a reverent spirit, and they were willing to permit considerable latitude in interpretations of theological doctrines. However, it was their contention that theology was moving in the direction of a naturalism which undermined the very gospel itself. "The issue is supernaturalism, pure and simple,"[17] insisted Dr. Laws again and again.

The moderate conservatives represented by Dr. Laws and Dr. Goodchild were willing that Baptists should have freedom to interpret the Scriptures for themselves. However, when theological interpretation involved a denial of the essential message of the Bible, it was time to protest. "The center of the controversy between the old and the new theologies," wrote Dr. Laws, "is the question of sin, of atonement, and of Christ's person."[18] It was around questions of sin and redemption, of man's predicament and of divine revelation, that the central message of the Scriptures revolved, and when these elements were imperiled, liberty of interpretation had overstepped its bounds.

If one wants to understand the Fundamentalists, it is necessary to look beyond individual issues to grasp their primary concern. To focus attention upon single points like the Virgin Birth, the authority of the Bible, the resurrection, the atonement, or the second coming is to be unable to see the forest because of the trees. The question of salvation is what is really at stake.

Much of the controversy between Fundamentalists and Modernists had to do with questions concerning the Bible, and therefore it is commonly said that the Fundamentalists were narrow literalists and bibliolatrists. While some conservatives were intent upon defending minute points, the more articulate voices of the Fundamentalists were mainly concerned to ensure that the core of the Biblical witness should be protected. They were not seeking to defend particular theories about the Bible, nor did they oppose Biblical criticism as such. "Fundamentalism," said Dr. Goodchild, "is not opposed to the most careful, most critical study of the Scriptures. But we do think that the study of God's Word, especially in our colleges and theological seminaries, should be reverent. We have no use for criticism whose evident purpose is destructive, and that leaves the impression on the student's mind that the Bible is nothing but a piece of human literature, and a bungled piece at that." [19] Nor was the issue simply one of inerrancy or infallibility. For example, Dr. Laws could say: "The infallibility of the Bible is the infallibility of common sense, and of the experimental triumph in us. We do not ask it about chemistry or astronomy or the constitution of matter, or the expansive power of gases, just as we do not ask a compass to tell us the time of the day, or predict the weather. The living power of the Bible is due to its living function in man's religious life." [20]

The Bible occupied a conspicuous place in the controversy because it is the source to which the Christian Church must go for a word about man's salvation. To treat these Scriptures with irreverence is to undermine the only witness to God's revelation; and to doubt either the deity or the saving work of Jesus Christ is to be left adrift without any basis for hope of salvation. Therefore, when a skeptical naturalism expressed doubts about the clear teachings of the Scriptures, voices of protest were raised. The Virgin Birth was important primarily as a touchstone which indicated whether a man was a naturalist or a supernaturalist, for it was clearly taught in the Bible and the only apparent reason for questioning the authenticity of the records was a reluctance to admit the miraculous intervention of God in human affairs. It seemed evident to conservatives that those who doubted what the Bible stated plainly were usually those who spurned all miracles *per se,* who denied Christ's deity, and who believed that man was outgrowing sin and did not really have need of a Savior other than one who furnished an example for others to follow. Over against the rationalists, or naturalists, stood those who believed the redemptive message of the Bible, who accepted the miraculous birth, the teachings and miracles of Jesus, the atoning death, the resurrection, and the hope of Christ's return to bring history to its culmination some day. To the Fundamentalist the lines of cleavage seemed very clear; the issue, pure and simple, was supernaturalism versus rationalism; and what was at stake was the ultimate question as to whether or not God had really spoken a saving word in Jesus Christ.

It is significant that a man of the stature of Dr. Augustus H. Strong considered the purpose and spirit of the Fundamentalists as expressive of his own sentiments. While the retired President, who had reached eighty-four years in 1920, could not participate actively in the movement, he did put himself on record as in sympathy with its aims. Having read accounts of the Buffalo conference in the newspapers he had gotten the impression that it must be a narrowly conservative movement. He had, therefore, declined to write a foreword to the printed proceedings of that conference when requested to do so by Dr. J. C. Massee. The newspaper accounts had played up statements of Dixon and Riley, and their attacks on evolution and Biblical criticism annoyed him. "I have always held that there is a theistic evolution," he wrote; and he added, "higher criticism has its rights, and instead of denouncing it, we must concede that it has thrown valuable light upon the methods employed in the composition of the Scripture." Later when he had read the published addresses, he found that their general tenor was in harmony with his own outlook. Therefore, he declared himself in favor of their theological position and their proposals to rid the schools of avowed Modernists as well as to have a doctrinal statement adopted by the Convention.[21]

It was at the Buffalo Convention in 1920 that the Fundamentalists began their concerted efforts to rid the Convention of noxious weeds. This meeting "witnessed the first line up . . . between the liberals and the conservatives," and the issue which divided them was a motion to investigate the denominational schools. A resolution to this end had been brought before the Convention upon recommendation of the preconvention conference. "The resolution looking to the investigation of the teaching in our schools, colleges, and seminaries created the wildest disorder," reported *The Watchman-Examiner*. "A sober, reverential, thoughtful body of men and women was transformed into a shouting, hissing, applauding bedlam. The behavior was shameful, but it is easily accounted for. The school question is the fundamental question." [22]

It was natural that a first move of the Fundamentalists should have been in the direction of scrutinizing the seminaries and colleges, for these are strategic points in the life of a denomination. The professors in the seminaries and the teachers of Bible in the colleges are the ones who are primarily entrusted with the task of preparing ministers. Such schools have the difficult job of serving as the intellectual centers of the denomination's life. They must pass on the tradition which has been handed down to them, but at the same time they are responsible for criticizing older interpretations in the light of new discoveries. Presenting the gospel effectively to contemporaries involves an inescapable double risk, either of letting the gospel become hardened in its moulds and irrelevant, or of permitting an over-accommodation which undermines the fundamentals. Hence, the seminary is both the source which needs to be kept free from pollution and the place where there is the most likelihood of locating trends toward unorthodoxy. The school situation, accordingly, was called "the fundamental question," and the first approach toward checking liberalism was a proposal to investigate the schools.

After the tumult had died down, the Convention voted that a committee should examine the schools and report back next year. The chairman of the committee was Dr. Frank Goodchild, who enjoyed the confidence of all factions in the denomination. The others were moderate conservatives, among whom was Dr. Austen K. de Blois. Contrary to the expectations of many, the report made at Des Moines the next year was generally favorable to the schools. It stated:

> "The committee is confident that for the most part our schools of all grades are doing a work of which the denomination may well be proud. Here and there doubtless is a teacher who has departed from the Baptist faith or has lost the Saviour's spirit. The utterances of these men have been published far and wide and have brought strife into our ranks and confusion to our work. It is the duty of the Baptist communities throughout the country to displace from the schools men who impugn the authority of the Scriptures as the Word of God and

who deny the deity of our Lord, but they must do it in the prescribed ways already indicated; and they ought to do it in such a way as will conserve the well-being of the churches which Christ has redeemed with his own blood, and in such a spirit as will extend and strengthen his work at home and abroad."[23]

The committee refrained from mentioning names of persons who they thought should be discharged, and the matter was left in the hands of the boards of trustees and the administrative officers. On the whole, both liberals and conservatives regarded the report as fair.

In the same year that the committee on schools reported, a second prong of the movement to safeguard orthodoxy took shape. This was an attempt to persuade the Northern Baptist Convention to adopt a doctrinal statement. The first step in that direction was the acceptance of such a statement by the pre-Convention conference on the fundamentals, and that action was taken in 1921.[24] There was nothing radical about the affirmations of that document, for it contained only what was generally held as orthodox by most Christians, except for the Baptist emphases of believers' baptism and the autonomy of the local church. Except for those two points, the statement would have been acceptable to all evangelical Christians.

So free of eccentricities was the Des Moines affirmation that many who did not belong to the movement expressed their approval of its contents. Professor A. S. Hobart of Crozer Seminary wrote in a letter to *The Baptist*: "Certainly there is the breadth of outdoors. The man who does not accept it all does not feel at home among Baptists."[25] In similar vein, Dean J. F. Vichert of Colgate Seminary expressed his agreeable surprise: "With much that has emanated from fundamentalist conventions I have no sympathy,

diminishing. However, before another year had passed a new controversy had developed. This centered around the American Baptist Foreign Mission Society. Instigated by Dr. John Roach Straton and the Fundamentalist League of Greater New York, a group affiliated with the Baptist Bible Union, there was an insistent demand for a full-scale probe of the missionaries of the Society. The Fundamentalists did not initiate this move, but when the accusations had been made, they lent support to the demand for a thorough examination of the faith and work of the missionaries. At first the Society resisted such a demand, but in the interests of harmony agreed to an investigation. The Convention of 1924, meeting at Milwaukee, authorized the appointment of a special commission for that purpose, and a representative body of Baptists carried out the assignment. The gist of the Committee's report at Seattle in 1925 was that with a few exceptions they had found little to criticize in the theology and ministry of the missionaries.[30] It was recommended that about eight persons be recalled for further examination, and the Society complied with the instructions, with the final result that about four of the eight were not returned to the mission field. Considering the size of the missionary force, the report was much better than might have been expected.

Of course, the more extreme elements cried out that there had been a whitewash of the whole affair. However, between the Convention sessions of 1924 and 1925, Dr. Curtis Lee Laws and Dr. Earle V. Pierce, both Fundamentalist leaders, had visited personally many of the mission fields. The results of their trip were published in the pages of *The Watchman-Examiner*[31] and helped to allay discontent and suspicion regarding the missionaries. Although Dr. Pierce noted that there were some signs of missionaries who were less evangelical than might be wished, he declared: "The great bulk of the missionary force is of heroic, hardworking, diligently praying, spiritually-minded and highly efficient evangels of the cross. As a class they are the cream of the Christian Church."

EASTERN SEMINARY LAUNCHED

Before the committee investigating the missionaries had reported in 1925, a decision had been taken to start a new seminary. Convinced that liberalism could not be checked in the older institutions and disturbed by the growth of Bible schools, a group of the Fundamentalists concluded that a new seminary should be established in the East. Numerous incidents occurred during the years between 1920 and 1925 which kept the contest between liberals and conservatives alive. For example, a book by a well known Baptist seminary professor had been published in 1922, and had caused considerable repercussion. In this volume he not only ridiculed the conservatives, but made such extreme statements as the following: "Paul appeals to a state of mind that has forever passed away—at least among civilized peoples, though his theology may still be helpful to African savages." [32] Also, Dr. Harry E. Fosdick had become a storm center in those years. Following the publication of his sermon, "Shall the Fundamentalists Win?" a train of events had led to his being forced out of the First Presbyterian Church of New York, where he had been supplying for several years. His frank espousal of modernism had agitated both Presbyterians and Baptists, and as plans were being projected for him to become pastor of the Park Avenue Baptist Church, which would be relocated and become an open-membership church, controversy continued to center around him. Numerous other incidents, some of which concerned the Divinity School of the University of Chicago, had led many people to the conviction that a new seminary was needed. Therefore, a seminary representing the wholesome conservatism of the Northern Baptist Fundamentalist movement was projected.

On March 19, 1925, the constituting meeting of The Eastern Baptist Theological Seminary was held. Most of the men who served as early trustees had been associated in the Fundamentalist conferences, and nearly all of the first faculty had taken part in the pre-Convention programs. There is a direct and strong link, then, between the movement which adopted the name "Fundamentalist" and Eastern. Hitherto, Dr. Laws had expressed confidence that the older schools could be recovered for orthodoxy, but now he agreed that another school was needed.

> "We have voiced our protest against certain teachings again and again. We propose to do it no more. Those in charge of the new seminary purpose founding a school of the prophets in which loyalty to the Scriptures shall be conspicuous. You will not get the impression when you visit its class rooms that they are cutting to pieces the Book that brought you the good news of your salvation and has been the unfailing source of your comfort and inspiration for many years. You will not come away feeling that the crown of deity has been taken off the brow of the One whom your soul adores." [33]

There has been a persistent misunderstanding of Eastern Seminary from the beginning, and the passing of time makes it all the more difficult to see that period in its true perspective. The school was the child of the Fundamentalists, but of a particular conservative group within the Northern Baptist Convention which adopted this term. When the leaders of this movement decided to found a new seminary, they did so because they discerned a peril to the gospel in the rampant liberalism of the day. It was their intention to establish an institution in which the essential elements of the Christian faith would be preserved, and which at the same time would represent an enlightened scholarship. Indeed, it may be fairly stated that the founders hoped to institute a school which would be conservative and progressive at the same time.

That their fears were not imaginary is acknowledged today by many who are not identified as conservatives. Professor Nels Ferré has written, "Fundamentalism as the defender of supernaturalism, has nevertheless a genuine heritage and a profound truth to preserve. If I may predict, I think that we shall some day thank our fundamentalist friends for having held the main fortress while countless leaders went over to the foe of a limited scientism and a shallow naturalism." [34] To say that liberalism constituted a threat to the gospel does not mean that we must discredit the men who honestly faced difficult issues courageously. Many liberals were devout Christians. However, having acknowledged this fact, we must say also that the Modernism with which these Fundamentalists contended has been largely disowned today.

The moderate conservative party out of which Eastern arose had its shortcomings too, but its leaders do not deserve the ridiculous charges which depict them as ignorant bigots. They belonged to a Fundamentalism which is not often described with accuracy today. It is difficult to make inclusive statements concerning the men who founded the school, for there was diversity of background and attitude among both trustees and faculty members. There were men of considerable breadth, like Dr. Laws and Dr. Goodchild; there also were laymen and pastors who were less well informed and who held narrower views. Within the faculty the levels of scholarly appreciation ranged from that of the erudite President de Blois to the more elementary and practical commonsense approach of the fatherly Dr. James A. Maxwell. There were various shades of opinion within their numbers, but the important point to note is the absence of men regarded as extremists, such as Drs. W. B. Riley, J. Frank Norris, and T. T. Shields.

Although not all of the trustees were like Drs. Laws and Goodchild, it is probably fair to see in these two a reflection of the spirit and ideals of Eastern at its best. Both of them had been among the most articulate voices of the Fundamentalist party from its beginning, and both had served in the early stages of planting the new theological institution. From what has already been said with regard to the opinions and attitudes of these men, it is possible to get some picture of their spirit. Perhaps an illustration or two may help to emphasize their peaceful temperament and co-operative spirit, which do not at all typify the pattern of fundamentalism as it is generally portrayed today.

An illustration which reveals the spirit of Dr. Goodchild is his review in 1925 of Dr. Fosdick's *The Modern Use of the Bible*. He wrote: "It is very difficult for one who knows and loves Dr. Harry Fosdick to review a book by him. . . . His personality is so engaging . . . his passionate love for Jesus Christ is so conspicuous that one is apt to think there can be nothing wrong with his teaching." [35] Then the reviewer proceeds to analyze the book and point out its modernistic tendencies. However, one can hardly picture the Fundamentalist as he is ordinarily caricatured today admitting that Dr. Fosdick had a "passionate love for Jesus Christ"!

A similar spirit was manifested by Dr. Laws, who was a champion of fair play. He spoke his mind forthrightly, but he offered the pages of *The Watchman-Examiner* to those who dissented from his views. To his mind, as he often said, the one real issue was that between supernaturalism and rationalism or naturalism, and he tried to avoid embroilments over secondary issues. That he did not equate acceptance of propositions with saving faith, as Fundamentalists are commonly said to do, is clear from his rejoinder to a man who argued that Modernists were not Christians since they did not believe the right doctrines. "We do not agree at all with the definition," he wrote. "To be a Christian means more than an intellectual assent to a prescribed scheme of things. The Christian is a man who through faith in Jesus Christ has received into his heart and life the Saviour's love, and who is directed in all matters of conduct, in the shaping of his character and in his intercourse with God and men, by the power of the Holy Ghost." [36]

There is no intention to convey the impression that the men who led the Fundamentalists were paragons of wisdom and virtue, for they had their faults like other men. What is meant is to exonerate them from false accusations of being narrow bigots, who treated the Bible with wooden literalism, were preoccupied with millennial programs, opposed social reforms, and championed narrow theories which they identified with orthodoxy. On the whole, they had a sense of the vital core of the gospel and maintained it in the face of a Modernism which in its desire to keep abreast of the times almost dissolved its message. Of course, not all Fundamentalists were as open-minded or as well informed as these men, but they were the accepted leaders and spokesmen, and represent the main thrust of organized Fundamentalism in the Northern Baptist Convention during the early 1920's.

The determined policy of the Eastern Baptist Seminary was to work within the Northern Baptist Convention. "The Seminary is to be conducted by loyal Baptist trustees and teachers," proclaimed the opening Statement of Policy. "Its function is to train Christian leaders . . . who shall be intelligent concerning Baptist principles and loyal to Baptist undertakings. . . . We believe that our Baptist work should be done through the denomination itself, and its constituted agencies." Moreover, the founders affirmed: "It is no part of our undertaking to engage in criticism and propaganda against other institutions." [37]

The ideal of Eastern was to be a school which would be at the same time both conservative and progressive. In an early bulletin, Dr. Gordon H. Baker expressed the aspirations of Eastern: "Too long have fundamentalism and ignorance been considered as synonymous terms. The board of trustees of The Eastern Baptist Theological Seminary desires to prove to the world that a man can accept the Bible as the Word of God and believe all the basic truths of Christianity and at the same time be a great scholar." [38] As one step toward the making of scholars, he proceeded to announce plans for making available graduate fellowships which would enable students to take doctoral work at the University of Pennsylvania, and for two annual fellowships for study in Europe.

At the outset, the trustees framed a Doctrinal Basis which would help to keep the seminary sound in theology. The attempt had been made to persuade the Convention to agree upon some such statement and had failed. Therefore, the trustees of the new institution saw that they would have to set forth the fundamentals of the faith in their own document, which they hoped would "guarantee the perpetual evangelical loyalty of this seminary." [39] Although the seminary has often been criticized for having a statement of doctrine which is subscribed to by its professors, there is nothing un-Baptistic in such a procedure, and those who drew it up showed great wisdom both in what they included and what they left out.

Careful scrutiny of the Doctrinal Basis will show that it aimed to protect the central verities of the gospel and the distinctive emphases of Baptists. Its affirmations are broad, but they set the limits within which freedom is possible. However the limits which are set are simply what the Church has held for centuries, except for the specifically Baptist views on baptism and the local church. Anyone who thinks that fundamentalism must be concerned particularly with the "five points" which are often supposed to summarize the interests of the group will be hard put to find them all in this document. Belief in the atonement of Christ is asserted, but it is said to be "vicarious" rather than "substitutionary." Indeed, a first draft had used the adjective "substitutionary," but it was omitted in the final writing in order to avoid the mechanical and crude interpretations which sometimes accompany that term. Belief in the authority of the Scriptures is stated, but there is affirmed thereby only what is held by all Protestants, and no attempt is made to state any particular theory of inspiration. Moreover, while belief in the return of Christ is declared, the writers took care not to commit the school to any given millennial position.

One of the significant indications of the purpose and spirit of Eastern is the selection of Dr. Austen K. de Blois as president, after one year under the leadership of Dr. Charles T. Ball. When he was called to the seminary, Dr. de Blois was serving as associate editor of *The Watchman-Examiner,* but he had had a distinguished career as an educator, pastor, scholar, and writer. A graduate of Acadia College, he had attended Newton Theological Institution, and held the M.A. and Ph.D. degrees from Brown University. In addition to graduate work at Brown, he had spent a year each at the

Universities of Leipzig and Berlin. Following his return to the United States, he became president of Shurtleff College, and then served in pastorates at the First Baptist Churches of Elgin, Chicago, and Boston. The list of important posts which he had filled in denominational activities is impressive, and at the time of his election to the presidency of Eastern he was still a trustee of Newton Theological Institution.

Some idea of the wide esteem in which he was held may be gained from the fact that even a Unitarian editor went out of his way to pay tribute to Dr. de Blois when he left Boston. In an editorial in the leading Unitarian periodical, it was stated: "Dr. de Blois is a man of grace and charm, of dignity and scholarship." The editor added: "He goes to a paper with which we have disagreed with all our might and soul in the great doctrinal issues of our time, but we have always respected it for giving no quarter in its stand for fundamentalism." This remark reveals that Dr. de Blois received praise from voices outside of his own denomination, and the fact that Dr. Laws reprinted a tribute from such a source reveals something of his spirit also.[40]

Always an independent thinker, Dr. de Blois had long upheld a large measure of academic freedom in the Baptist schools. Aware of the dangers inherent in a conservative movement, he urged, "Let us preserve an open-mind at all costs." [41] The champion of many causes, he had a strong social concern and a hopeful outlook upon society. In the latter connection he wrote: "The Church has maintained a dauntless enthusiasm for militant righteousness. . . . I believe in the upward movement of the ages. I believe that the tendencies of civilization are onward and Godward." [42] That the trustees should call such a man to help shape the new institution and to commend Eastern to the Northern Baptists discloses something of their own ideals. True, they expected him to help put the school on the map, but had they been narrower men, they would not have elected such a person to head the institution.

Possessed of a liberal spirit, President de Blois was nevertheless a conservative in theology, much in the tradition of Drs. Augustus H. Strong, Curtis Lee Laws, and Frank M. Goodchild. Called to be the head of the infant school, he aspired to direct its destiny toward the fulfillment of the trustees' hope that it should combine conservative theology with sound scholarship. He was impatient with tendencies toward lax standards of education, and he was often annoyed that people regarded Eastern as a glorified Bible school. "Let us talk straight!" he exclaimed to the trustees. He continued:

> "The purpose of our Seminary is to compete triumphantly with the modernist theological seminaries. To do so we must meet them on their own level in the educational field. We must give just as virile an intellectual discipline. We must prepare just as accurate a scholarship, and a scholarship much more sound. We must secure for our Baptist pastorates an ever-enlarging group of thoroughly trained men who shall be loyal in all things to Jesus Christ and the fundamentals of the Christian faith, and who shall be just as able, as scholarly, as intellectually equipped, and as devoted to sinewy intellectual labors, as the men who go forth from those schools which have lost their fair vision of an atoning Saviour." [43]

The selection of the faculty likewise reflected a desire to choose men who represented a sane and balanced conservatism. Anyone who was acquainted with the members of the early faculty would find it difficult to envision them in the role of "fighting" Fundamentalists. They were men of Christian culture, irenic in temper, active in denominational life, and dedicated to Christian service. They were men of conviction, but not proponents of weird emphases. It was their desire to provide the churches with ministers who had deep convictions rooted in the gospel of Jesus Christ, were evangelistic in spirit, and equipped to minister in various church callings. Eastern was indeed a Fundamentalist seminary, and its professors welcomed that label for themselves, but they represented a Fundamentalism which was vital, co-operative, fair-minded, and concerned about essentials.

From the standpoint of attitudes and theological position, the faculty represented a moderate conservatism, but they were not the men who could fulfill aspirations toward a high level of scholarship. As announced by Dr. Laws in the opening year, the professors were "men who have had long and honored careers as pastors of our churches, not men who have specialized in technical scholarship." [44] Although they were more practical men of affairs than technical scholars, they were not ignorant men and their academic preparation should not be discounted. Of the thirteen men who taught during the first two years, eight were graduates of both college and seminary, and four of their number had earned doctorates. The other five had served in the practical fields, but most of them had virtual equivalents of college and seminary training.

When one has taken note of the fairly high level of general education possessed by these professors, however, it must be said in all candor that they lacked the preparation needed to make the dream of Dr. de Blois and some of the trustees come true. Few of them had had experience in teaching or possessed specialized knowledge in any field. They were mostly older men whose experience had been largely pastoral and administrative. Not having lived in academic environments, most of them were not acutely aware of the pressing problems which perplexed theological studies. Undoubtedly, some assumed too easily that students could be brought to positive and intelligent convictions without tackling thorny questions. Consequently, they were sometimes too easy-going in their requirements, and they often tended to be over-protective toward their students, instead of forcing them to face up to the issues with which modernist seminaries were wrestling.

The desire to be both conservative and progressive led to tensions at many points. There were strange contrasts between open-mindedness and intolerance, and even the same individual might exhibit considerable ambivalence from one situation to another. Such contrast may be seen, for example, with regard to the use of textbooks. In the courses in Old and New Testament theology, Dr. Champion used as textbooks those by A. B. Davidson and G. B. Stevens, respectively, both of which frankly accepted the results of Higher Criticism. He also taught a venturesome and creative theory of the atonement, emphasizing what he called "the personal point of view," in contrast to more mechanical conceptions. On the other hand, when it was reported that a certain textbook being used in a Christian education course had objectionable views, it was voted that the books should be recalled and the students reimbursed. On one occasion, a trustee persuaded the board to require that books should not be put on the library shelves until they had been inspected by one of their number, but fortunately the administration of such a plan was unworkable.

A similar tension affected relationships with others. Although the school adhered to its avowed purpose to avoid criticism of other institutions and parties, the consciousness of being defenders of the faith involved a negative element which provided an important motivating force. There was a fairly consistent accent upon the positive mission of the school, but sometimes the public was reminded even by President de Blois: "The Eastern Baptist Theological Seminary was founded as a protest against the rationalistic and modernistic teaching in existing Baptist seminaries. Let this fact be definitely and tenaciously held in mind." [45]

The Eastern Seminary professors did not foment strife or cultivate suspicious attitudes toward the Convention. Although some alumni have joined in secessionist movements from the denomination, they did not receive encouragement from the seminary to do so. Unwittingly, the school may have encouraged the sharpening of party lines by a neglect to deal more forthrightly with problems. There was undoubtedly much oversimplification of issues in the early seminary courses, and graduates often saw issues in terms of black and white without any intermediate shades of gray. That fact made it easier to label dissenters as liberals and to cut off fellowship with them. Moreover, without the ability to come to grips intelligently with great problems, alumni could not engage in any genuine dialogue with people who represented contrary points of view. The consequence was that party lines were strengthened, and liberal and conservative groups within the denomination became more isolated from each other. In this way the school possibly contributed to the isolation of liberal and conservative elements, who for years had little communication with each other.

Some strain has been felt with regard to theological changes which have taken place over the past thirty-five years. The altered climate of thought has posed problems for a school which has sought to conserve the vital elements from the past and also to take cognizance of new light which is granted to men. It is characteristic of conservatism that it tends to assume that all of the important questions have been settled, and hence resists attempts to re-examine old terms and formulations of doctrine. It was this inclination which Dr. de Blois had in mind when he warned against the tendency to "petrify truths in the form of propositions." Knowing the constant danger that a "healthy conservatism" may become sick and a wholesome conservatism become a dead orthodoxy, he pleaded for an open mind.

It was a difficult thing that the founders of Eastern tried to do—to be both conservative and progressive. In that attempt, however, they were doing only what the Church has always been called upon to do. The Word of God must always be spoken to a contemporary generation in relevant terms, but in a way which does not neglect or destroy the fundamentals of the faith, for these are not subject to change. In that process it is often difficult to distinguish between the words which embody our perceptions of reality and the reality itself. The Fundamentalists of the Northern Baptist Convention were seeking to be true to the heritage of the gospel without being indifferent to their times. Believing that the reductionist tendencies of Modernism would throw out the baby with the bath, they concluded that a seminary should be organized which would combine the essential witness of the gospel with the developments of modern knowledge. At some points, they succeeded in fulfilling their intentions; at others, they made mistakes which are clearer to hindsight than they could have been to them. Eastern still seeks to carry on this original purpose of the Fundamentalists, and struggles with the tensions inherent in the attempt to be both conservative and progressive. In the process of seeking to be loyal to the Word of God and to be relevant to our times, the spirit of the founders, the Doctrinal Basis, and the living tradition constituted by our alumni have helped to maintain the heritage of Eastern and to keep it vital and alert.

NOTES

1. *Bulletin of the E. B. T. S.*, Vol. 1, No. 1 (1925).
2. *Christian Century*, May 28, 1925, p. 712.
3. *The Baptist*, May 9, 1925, p. 435.
4. Norman Furniss, *The Fundamentalist Controversy*, 1918-1931 (New Haven: Yale University Press, 1954).
5. *Bulletin of Fuller Theological Seminary*, Oct.-Dec., 1954.
6. E. J. Carnell, *A Handbook of Christian Theology*, pp. 142-143.
7. E. B. Hulbert, "The Baptist Outlook," in *The English Reformation and Puritanism: With Other Lectures and Addresses*, p. 441.
8. *Watchman-Examiner*, Oct. 31, 1918, pp. 1357-1358.
9. A. H. Strong, *A Tour of the Missions*, pp. 190-191.
10. *Watchman-Examiner*, May 20, 1920, p. 652.
11. *Ibid.*, July 1, 1920, p. 834.
12. F. M. Goodchild, "The Fundamentalists and the Bible Union," *Watchman-Examiner*, Oct. 22, 1925, pp. 1361-1362. See also C. L. Laws, "The Fundamentalists and the Bible Union," *ibid.*, April 19, 1923, pp. 486-488.
13. C. L. Laws, "Teaching Evolution in the Schools," *ibid.*, July 2, 1925, p. 845.
14. *Ibid.*, July 1, 1920, p. 834; April 21, 1921, p. 488. See also "Premillennialism Not the Issue," *ibid.*, May 10, 1923, pp. 581-582.
15. C. L. Laws, "The Fundamentalists Still Misunderstood," *ibid.*, Aug. 20, 1925, p. 1071.
16. F. M. Goodchild, "What the Fundamentalists Stand For," *ibid.*, Dec. 10, 1925, pp. 1587-1588.
17. "The War in the Churches," *ibid.*, Nov. 15, 1923, pp. 1453-1454.
18. *Ibid.*, March 29, 1917, p. 390; see also March 12, 1925, pp. 325-326; and Oct. 8, 1925, pp. 1293-1294.
19. *Ibid.*, March 2, 1922, p. 268.
20. *Ibid.*, Feb. 1, 1917, p. 134; see also Nov. 4, 1920, p. 1349.
21. *Ibid.*, July 21, 1921, p. 910.
22. *Ibid.*, July 1, 1920, p. 834.
23. *Ibid.*, July 7, 1921, p. 842.
24. *Ibid.*, July 30, 1921, p. 805.
25. *Ibid.*, July 28, 1921, p. 944.
26. *Ibid.*, March 2, 1922, pp. 266-267.
27. *Ibid.*, June 29, 1922, pp. 814-816; July 27, 1922, p. 946.
28. *Ibid.*, June 12, 1924, p. 738.
29. *Ibid.*, June 7, 1923, p. 706.
30. *Ibid.*, May 28, 1925, pp. 689-693.
31. *Ibid.*, May 21, 1925, pp. 645-646, 657-659.
32. H. C. Vedder, *Fundamentals of Christianity*, p. 190.
33. *Watchman-Examiner*, June 18, 1925, p. 781.

34. Nels S. F. Ferré, "Present Trends in Protestant Thought," in *Religion in Life* (1948), p. 335.
35. *Watchman-Examiner,* Feb. 19, 1925, pp. 235-237.
36. *Ibid.,* Jan. 7, 1926, p. 7.
37. *Bulletin of the E. B. T. S.,* Vol. 1, No. 1 (1925).
38. *Ibid.,* June 1, 1930, pp. 59-60.
39. *Ibid.,* Vol. 1, No. 1 (1925).
40. *Watchman-Examiner,* Jan. 28, 1926, p. 105.
41. *Ibid.,* March 19, 1925, p. 365.
42. *Ibid.,* Sept. 24, 1925, p. 1234.
43. *Minutes, Board of Trustees,* April 27, 1928, pp. 169-171.
44. *Watchman-Examiner,* Nov. 19, 1925, p. 1487.
45. *Bulletin of E. B. T. S.,* Vol. 2, No. 4, p. 16 (1927).

II

THE FORMATIVE YEARS

by

GORDON H. BAKER

THE HISTORY OF The Eastern Baptist Theological Seminary is a romance in Christian education. In this story there is fast-moving, thrilling, compelling drama. The record cannot be adequately given in a few brief chapters. In a survey such as this must be, many important persons and events cannot even be mentioned.

The progress of Eastern has been remarkable. From the very beginning the blessings of God were upon the trustees and faculty as they tried to develop a school with high scholastic standards, doctrinal soundness, and denominational loyalty. To safeguard the doctrinal integrity of the school a brief statement of faith was adopted at the beginning, to be signed annually by the members of the faculty and the board of trustees. Eastern sought to make the Bible the center of its curriculum, and evangelism the core of its activities. The trustees believed in progressive education, but not the kind promoted by some liberals of that day. They knew that only the tree whose roots go down deep in the soil will be able to stand against the storms. So they attempted to build Eastern Seminary on a solid and sure foundation, and, at the same time, to allow ample room for sane intellectual expansion. They wanted to prove to the world that a man can be a scholar and still believe the Bible to be the word of God.

While there was an element of protest in the minds of the founders against the modernism of that day, Eastern was not founded simply or mainly as a protest institution. It was not the purpose of the trustees or faculty to conduct a propaganda of criticism against other institutions of learning, but to develop a constructive program of Christian education. There was a vacuum in the theological world. Many of the young men sent out to preach, by some of the leading seminaries, did not proclaim a virile and effective gospel. The churches were clamoring for men with a real, vital, redeeming message from God, and Eastern was organized to meet that need.

Bible schools were springing up in all directions, but they were meeting the need only in part. Some of these Bible schools were good, but not good enough. They took students who had very little education to start with and failed to give them the culture and training that would make them wise and successful pastors and leaders. This is no reflection on the work done at the Bible schools. They were not set up to give a general education. Many of them were poorly equipped and inadequately financed. The need for a high grade conservative theological seminary here in the East was very great.

The Eastern Baptist Theological Seminary was organized on March 19, 1925, in the building of the American Baptist Publication Society, 1701 Chestnut Street, Philadelphia. Six ministers were present at the first meeting; they were Charles

T. Ball, Harry Watson Barras, Groves W. Drew, Ralph L. Mayberry, John A. Hainer, and Gordon H. Baker. No one present that day realized the importance of that meeting. All of those present, except Dr. Drew, agreed to act as trustees. Others elected to the board on that occasion were: James A. Maxwell, David Lee Jamison, Frank Earle Parham, John E. Briggs, Curtis Lee Laws, Frank M. Goodchild, and Thornley B. Wood.

DR. CHARLES T. BALL

Dr. Goodchild was elected chairman of the board of trustees, and the Rev. Charles T. Ball, president of the Seminary. An executive committee was appointed consisting of Drs. Ball, Barras, Maxwell, Hainer, and Mayberry. Dr. Mayberry was chosen as secretary and Dr. Barras as treasurer. That was the simple organization of the first day. Later that year several other persons were added to the board of trustees; namely, E. B. Dwyer, William P. Haug, Ralph I. Levering, Wesley H. Hoot, all of Pennsylvania; William H. Waite, Rhode Island; P. V. Slawter, New Jersey; Henry W. Munger, J. B. Champion, and Lawrence N. Sirrell, New York; Joseph Y. Erwin, Maryland; Mrs. Carl R. Gray, Nebraska; and Alonzo R. Stark, Ohio.

Without doubt, the organizing genius of Eastern Seminary was Dr. Charles T. Ball. He was a natural promoter and a man of unusual ability who had had considerable experience in promoting youth movements in the South. He was ably assisted by Drs. Barras, Maxwell, Hainer, and others in the Philadelphia area. The task before these men was tremendous. A building had to be secured, teachers chosen, the school incorporated, a statement of faith prepared, a curriculum developed, by-laws prepared and adopted, and many other details worked out. So far there was nothing but a board of trustees, a set of officers, an executive committee, a great idea, unusual enthusiasm, and a conquering faith.

Eastern had no money—not one cent. Dr. Barras was engaged at $20 a Sunday to visit the churches and plead the school's cause. Dr. Hainer's church, the Blockley Baptist Church, Philadelphia, was the first to send in a gift. It was in the amount of $26.00. But what can you do with such a gigantic task and only $26.00 to finance it? The Board proceeded, however, on the assumption that money would be available. At a meeting of the trustees held on May 28, 1925, only two months after the seminary was organized, Dr. Maxwell made the amazing statement that a man and his wife in California had made a gift of twenty thousand shares of stock worth more than a half million dollars, and a promise of more to follow.

Originally the trustees intended to engage a Sunday school room in some downtown church for class purposes, to engage local pastors as part-time teachers, and to use a room in the Publication Society's building for headquarters. They expected to have, that first year, a student body of from twelve to fifteen. But, with the receipt of this generous gift and the promise of more, the whole picture was changed. The trustees bought a building on South Rittenhouse Square, in downtown Philadelphia. Soon they bought another. The student body during the first school year reached one hundred. There were nine full-time professors and six instructors. The professors were: Drs. Charles T. Ball, Barnard C. Taylor, W. W. Adams, Harry Watson Barras, David Lee Jamison, Arthur E. Harris, Wilber T. Elmore, George W. Swope, and John B. Champion. All of these were able and consecrated men. The instructors were: Mrs. W. T. Elmore,

Boyce Hudson Moody, Mrs. C. Harold Thompson, Edward K. Worrell, L. Sarle Brown, and Grace R. Vanaman.

The Seminary started with four schools: the School of Theology, the School of Religious Education, the School of Missions, and the School of Sacred Music. The most difficult task of the first year was the building of a workable curriculum. Such a problem cannot be solved in a day or even in a year. The faculty had a curriculum committee of which Professor W. W. Adams was the chairman. The trustees also had a curriculum committee. These two committees worked in complete harmony with each other; but no person who has not had experience can understand the problems involved. To harmonize the constant conflicts in hours, in courses, in classes, and in classrooms requires time and study, patience and perseverance, adjustments and re-adjustments, and even then the perfect answer may not be found.

In December, 1925, the State Council of Education sent one of its representatives from Harrisburg to Philadelphia to examine the Seminary and its equipment. After a thorough investigation of classes, officers, faculty, trustees, scholastic standing, and preparations, the Seminary was granted authority to confer the following degrees: B.Th., B.D.; Th.M.; Th.D.; and D.D. To obtain the right to grant these degrees only eight months after the organization of the Seminary was unique in the history of religious education in the State of Pennsylvania.

Thus the first year of Eastern's history was one of marvelous progress. A charter had been obtained, two buildings had been purchased, a faculty secured, by-laws adopted, a statement of faith approved, the right to grant degrees obtained, and the building of a curriculum begun. At the first annual meeting of the board of trustees, held in May, 1926, Ralph I. Levering, chairman of the finance committee, reported investments, to the amount of $989,140.87. Dr. Barras, the treasurer, reported that about $13,000 had been received from the churches. The student aid fund had received $5,076. Here was the foundation and the beginning of what has proved to be one of the great theological seminaries in America.

The road to progress, however, is never in a straight line. There was confusion, and tragedy too. The pathway to success must often be trodden with bleeding feet and aching hearts. First, there was tragedy. Dr. George W. Swope, the much-loved professor of Evangelism, was taken from the school by death, March 17, 1926. He was an able and deeply consecrated Christian. The Seminary could ill afford to lose him so early in its history; but since the trustees believed God and accepted His promises, they knew He would guide them in choosing a worthy successor. There was also confusion. President Ball was a skillful promoter and deserves considerable credit for the leadership he gave and the work he did. As the months passed however, it became increasingly evident, both to the faculty and to the trustees, that the school needed a more effective administrator. Therefore, at the first annual meeting of the board of trustees, Dr. Austin Kennedy de Blois of New York was elected president. The trustees wanted Dr. Ball to remain with the seminary as a promoter of its interests, but he declined. Several years later he founded Eastern University, a school never connected with the Seminary, which closed after a few years of operation. Thus ended the first year of Eastern's remarkable history.

DR. AUSTIN KENNEDY de BLOIS

For ten years (1926-1936) Dr. Austin K. de Blois led The Eastern Baptist Theological Seminary in a program of steady progress. At the end of the first year Eastern's organization was fairly well established, but it had little recognition in the Baptist denomination or in the eyes of the general public. Many people did not know that Eastern existed. Many others who did know of its existence regarded Eastern as a "glorified Bible school."

The great need was a leader who could guarantee the Seminary a place among the standard schools of higher education. Dr. de Blois filled that need magnificently. When he became president the outlook of Eastern changed immediately and impressively. He was a man of scholarly habits and of wide influence far beyond Baptist circles. He was also a man of experience: formerly president of a Baptist theological seminary in St. Martins, New Brunswick, Canada, and later of Shurtleff College, Alton, Illinois. He had been the successful pastor of the First Baptist Church, Chicago, Illinois, and later of the First Baptist Church, Boston, Massachusetts. At the time of his call to become president of Eastern, he was associate editor, with Dr. Curtis Lee Laws, of the *Watchman-Examiner,* a national Baptist paper with headquarters in New York.

Soon after he accepted the position of president of Eastern he announced the following policy: "My purpose in the conduct of this institution, already so highly honored of God, and prosperous, is five-fold: (1) To enthrone the English Bible at the heart of our many-sided work, central to all our studies and efforts. (2) To emphasize evangelism as the attitude and end of our teaching service and practical activities. (3) To provide complete and scholarly training in all departments of a first class and well-rounded theological curriculum. (4) To seek constantly the direct guidance of the Holy Spirit, that the missionary passion may empower our plans and labors. (5) To serve our great denomination with unswerving loyalty." We quote this statement of purpose here because it was in complete harmony with the aims of the founding trustees, and Eastern has not deviated from this position in thirty-five years. Of course, much has been added to it, but the general purpose and outline remain the same.

One of the first things Dr. de Blois sought to do was to educate the public with regard to Eastern. He visited colleges, universities, and theological seminaries, where he spoke to professors and students. His purpose was not merely to get students, though many of them came to Eastern as a result of his visits, but to make Eastern known as a theological seminary of high standing. He told of its scholarship, equipment, and high spiritual aims. The professors, and especially Dr. Barras, Dr. Adams, Dr. Jamison, and Dr. Elmore, likewise helped to tell Eastern's wonderful story. His leadership did much to secure the recognition of Eastern by the Board of Education of the Northern Baptist Convention. This resulted in a listing of the Seminary among the convention schools of higher education. In a comparatively short time many people were sounding the praises of Eastern from the Atlantic to the Pacific.

While this was a great service and very much needed, his greatest achievements were accomplished on the inside. He had to find some new professors and to make new adjustments in the curriculum. There was the matter of discipline to be supervised; the students had to be fed, and in the early days of the Seminary this presented a considerable problem. The library had to be built up, and there were scores of other internal affairs to be promoted, adjusted, and supervised.

Dr. Herbert F. Stilwell was called to the chair of Evangelism to succeed Dr. George W. Swope. Dr. Stilwell formerly had been secretary of evangelism for the Home Mission Society of the Northern Baptist Convention. He was a tower of strength to Eastern; a man of keen intellect, strong personality, wealth of experience, and a lovable disposition. Dr. James A. Maxwell was called as professor of the English Bible. What a marvelous choice this proved to be! He was an unusual man whose record will never be adequately written. He was an outstanding executive, and a popular teacher. Because of his influence, the chair of English Bible was endowed so that his name will be perpetuated in the history of Eastern Seminary. Dr. George F. Wortley, who had just received a doctor of philosophy degree from Boston University, was called to head the School of Religious Education. In the fall of 1927, at the recommendation of Dr. de Blois, Professor John Barton Turner of England, a man well recommended by Dr. Thomas Phillips and Dr. John C. Carlisle as having rare gifts and scholastic training, was temporarily engaged to teach at Eastern.

With the vacancies on the faculty filled, the president set himself to the task of expanding and adjusting the curriculum. Dr. W. W. Adams was the chairman of the curriculum committee and upon his shoulders rested the responsibility for producing a workable plan. With him, working in close fellowship, were Dr. Barras, Dr. Elmore, and the president.

Students kept pouring into Eastern. By October 1, 1927, 120 students had registered, and more were to follow. It may be safely said that never before in Baptist history in the North had any theological school enrolled 120 students for full-time gospel training within two weeks of the opening of the second year of its history. Miss Irene Jones was engaged for one year (1934) as dean of women. So acceptable were her services that she was retained year after year. In 1938 she was elected a member of the faculty. She remained until May, 1943, when she resigned to accept a call to become home base secretary of the Woman's American Baptist Foreign Mission Society. Dr. Jones contributed much to the spirit and progress of Eastern.

Reference must now be made to a young man of brilliant mind and balanced judgment who was destined to become a leader in the life of Eastern Seminary. No student ever entered Eastern who does not know Professor Carl H. Morgan. He started as a student at the Seminary in 1926. In 1927 he became a teacher in the School of Music; then a teacher of New Testament Greek. In 1932 when the Pre-theological Department was introduced, he became its leader. Following the resignation of Professor Gorham, he was elected to be the head of the School of Religious Education. Finally, when Dr. Adams resigned to become president of Central Baptist Theological Seminary, Kansas City, Kansas, Dr. Morgan took his place as professor of New Testament Interpretation and Greek. In the meantime, he had obtained his doctor of philosophy degree from the University of Pennsylvania. Dr. Morgan is one of the most versatile men we have ever had at Eastern. He has filled many important positions in the school. In addition to being a teacher, and he is one of the best, he has served as dean since that office was established in May, 1940. He was for many years chairman of the student aid committee. His willingness to serve wherever he has been needed and to carry an extra load most of the time, and to do so without complaint, is a characteristic that has marked his pathway through the thirty-five years of Eastern's history. A few years ago the Seminary celebrated a quarter of a century of Dr. Morgan's teaching at Eastern, an honor which he well deserved.

Harry Watson Barras was one of the founders of Eastern. After spending some years in the pastorate, he became a secretary for the American Baptist Publication Society. When

Eastern Seminary was organized he became the professor of Homiletics, the treasurer, and the first dean. He carried a heavy load and did it cheerfully. When Dr. de Blois was absent on vacation, Dr. Barras stood by and cared for the correspondence and registrations. How deserving of special mention were all the professors who served during the regime of Dr. de Blois! Indeed, all of the men connected with Eastern, whether on the faculty, in the administration, or on the board of trustees had three aims in common: high scholarship for the students, a deep spiritual experience for themselves, and a consuming concern on the part of all for the salvation of the lost. That is why Eastern, early in its history, adopted the motto: "The whole gospel for the whole world."

THE SCHOOL OF RELIGIOUS EDUCATION

The School of Religious Education (in 1935 its name was changed to the School of Christian Education) at first was directed by Dr. George F. Wortley. He resigned in 1930, and Dr. Donald R. Gorham was elected to be his successor. The work in this school is closely related to that in the School of Theology and in the School of Missions.

Religious education is not something new, but the emphasis placed upon it and the methods used to promote it in our churches are new. Never before have churches been so aware of the need and value of planned religious education as they have been in the last fifty years. Previously people in our churches depended for their instruction upon pulpit messages and what they could learn from the Sunday school; but now we have discovered that it is the function of the whole church to educate. Someone has said, "Evangelization without education is evaporation." Today we have released-time schools, vacation schools, week-day Bible schools, schools of missions, Bible conferences, and many other methods of religious instruction.

Many churches have a board of education which plans, develops, and directs the educational program for the whole church. Some of the larger churches employ one or more trained directors to execute these plans. It is assumed that the director of Christian education in a church will be as well trained for his work as is the teacher in the public school. In any case, the pastor is the key-man in every church. Whether or not he has a trained director to assist him, he must have adequate knowledge of the value of Christian education to the church and of the best methods to be used in building a strong educational program.

For many years churches had been searching for well-trained religious education leaders and could not find them. At the time Eastern was founded, not a single theological school in the North was preparing students for this task. Eastern was the first to have a department devoted particularly to the training of students to meet this need. This school has done a tremendous work. More will be said about it in another chapter.

THE SCHOOL OF MISSIONS

The founders of Eastern prayed passionately that the new seminary would always be strongly missionary in its spirit and teaching. They knew that Eastern was founded at a time when vast changes were taking place in every department of life, in all parts of the world. They recognized that new conditions and new challenges were demanding up-to-date training for the modern missionary. Evidently the Spirit of God guided them in choosing Dr. Wilber T. Elmore to head this school. Dr. Elmore graduated from the University of Nebraska and Rochester Theological Seminary. He received his Ph.D. from the University of Nebraska and his honorary degree of D.D. from Colgate University. He had been a missionary to India under the American Baptist Foreign Mission Society from 1900 to 1915; and professor for six years in Ramapatnam Theological Seminary. He was a source of intellectual and spiritual power at Eastern. Mrs. Elmore became a valuable instructor on missionary topics in the Seminary. Under the leadership of Dr. Elmore, the missionary spirit grew and missionary information was increased. Eastern has provided an unusually large number of missionaries to the home and foreign fields of our denomination. Moreover the pastors trained at Eastern have a missionary passion and are able to lead their churches in developing a strong program of missionary education. The church that does not have a world-wide vision can never continue to be a growing church. An important part of Eastern's task is to train men and women in the knowledge of missions, to give them a world vision, and to send them out to be real missionaries, whether they become pastors or missionaries working under some board of our denomination.

THE SCHOOL OF MUSIC

Eastern was fortunate in securing as head of this school, Professor L. Sarle Brown. He was one of the original teachers, engaged when Dr. Charles T. Ball was president. He knew the value of musical training to the ministry and to the churches. He sought to make the School of Music the best in the country. Perhaps the best evidence of his success was the fact that many of his students became song-leaders in their churches, at associational gatherings, and at state conventions. The choirs he developed at the Seminary went up and down the eastern section of America inspiring the churches with their songs and testimonies. In the development of this school, Professor Brown had the able assistance of Joseph R. Bowman, Mrs. W. Theodore Taylor, Virginia Snyder, Marguerite Sibley, Daisy Adams Brown, Emily Stokes Hagar, Mary M. Kindleberger, Carl H. Morgan, Nettie Beatrice Hugar, Marion V. Jayne, David Christiansen, H. Alexander Matthews, Marion L. Stein, Maxine Anderson, and several others.

Joseph R. Bowman came to Eastern as a student in the Music Department. He soon became associated with Professor Brown in teaching music. Mr. Brown taught voice and church music and Professor Bowman taught choral literature and conducting. When in 1953 Professor Brown resigned to accept a position with the Southwestern Baptist Theological Seminary, Seminary Hill, Texas, Professor Bowman became head of the Music Department. Since that date, most of this work has been incorporated in the curriculum of Eastern Baptist College.

THE LIBRARY

Another important development under the leadership of Dr. de Blois was the growth of the seminary library. Eastern started the first year with a small collection of books. Their value was limited and they were not catalogued. It was recognized that no school of higher education could be strong unless adequately equipped with a good library. In building Eastern's library Dr. de Blois rendered exceptional service. He was heart and soul in favor of a strong library for Eastern. On his frequent trips to Europe he purchased hundreds of volumes, some of ancient origin and some modern books.

THE EXTENSION DEPARTMENT

It was the desire of the trustees and the faculty to extend the influence of Eastern Seminary as far as possible. They decided at the very beginning to conduct a Correspondence School. By this means they could reach many pastors and Christian workers who were unable to attend the classes at the Seminary. These people could not come to Eastern, but Eastern could go to them. They studied the courses sent to them, passed the examinations, and received certificates covering the work done. Several state conventions, including that of Pennsylvania, endorsed these correspondence courses and urged many of their pastors to use this method of instruction. Professor A. E. Harris was chosen by the faculty and elected by the trustees to take charge of this department of the educational program. These extension courses were conducted for about twenty years with excellent success. When they finally were discontinued, it was due to the accelerated war program (1943-1945) and to the impossibility of granting credits under the Pennsylvania law.

THE SUMMER SCHOOL

In its youthful vigor Eastern refused to close its eyes to any worthwhile opportunity for Christian service. Demands were coming in from various quarters that a Summer School be started. Eastern gladly responded, and at the close of the second year a Summer School of five weeks duration was started. Courses were offered in English Bible, Christian Doctrine, Church History, Missions, Homiletics, Evangelism, and Religious Education. Credits were given to students who took the regular courses and passed the examinations when the studies were completed. Students who did not want to work for credits were classified as "special students" and were not required to take the examinations. This school was open to both men and women. Regular students could attend the Summer School and gain credits for themselves on their Seminary work. Local and nearby pastors who could attend the morning sessions came to this school. Prospective students who wanted to give the Seminary a trial before enrolling as regular students could do so by attending this school. The Seminary found this another way to extend its influence. The summer session operated for a few years, then was closed until 1951 when it was re-established. It continues today with splendid acceptance.

PREACHING EFFECTIVENESS

Dr. de Blois considered it a weakness in the curriculum that more attention was not given to the delivery of the sermon. He insisted that adequate provision should be made for careful instruction in the art of preaching. He said:

"Important as are all our disciplines for ministerial success and complete educational development, there is no subject that has more vital and continuing value for the minister than an efficient training in this department.

"Ministers may be learned in Hebrew, Greek, Theology, and Psychology, in the annals of the church's past and in the approved methods of the church's outlook upon the world; but unless the preacher has the power of reaching the heart of his hearers, he fails in his ministry. The preacher is still needed, and he is needed today as he never has been needed in the past.

"We are training men to think, and to think truly, and to think toward substantial and accurate conclusions. We are teaching them to develop study habits. We are teaching them the elements of critical research so that they may become valiant seekers after truth. We are teaching them to understand and evaluate the history of the Christian church. We are teaching them the elements of the great and ancient languages in which the Bible was written down for the enlightenment of mankind. All this is well, and all this is necessary; but unless this erudite and accomplished man is able to stand up in the face of a congregation and deliver a message from God in forceful and awakening terms, we have missed our mark and we have helped him to miss his."

All the members of the faculty and all the trustees would say "amen" to this emphatic pronouncement. It indicates the high goals set at Eastern. Even though those goals were never fully reached, they show that the Seminary was pressing on toward perfection.

PRACTICAL WORK

Evangelism will never be a dead cause so long as The Eastern Baptist Theological Seminary exists. It is the core of its thinking and acting. It permeates and influences everything it says and does. The story of salvation through Jesus Christ is learned in the classroom, but the story must be told. Students do not wait until they graduate to tell the story. Some of them become student pastors. Some teach in the Sunday schools in the Philadelphia area. Some do street preaching and distribute evangelistic literature. Some conduct prayer meetings. Some visit prisons and hospitals, and in scores of other ways make the gospel story known. To get the best results, this clinical work of the students needed to be planned and supervised. This was part of the function of the Department of Evangelism.

Under such leaders as Drs. H. F. Stilwell, B. T. Livingston, and Albert G. Williams, this practical work has grown into a project of deep meaning and great value to both the students and to the Seminary. Through it the students gain experience as well as knowledge, while at the same time they render a very valuable service to the Kingdom of God. To read one of the monthly reports of this department will amaze and thrill any Christian and reveal the scope of the students' activities.

PUBLICITY

To record the history of the Seminary and make it known to others, a small bulletin was published several times a year, one issue of which was the annual catalogue. In 1932 the *Christian Review* was published. It appeared four times a year and was edited by Dr. de Blois. Dr. A. E. Harris was the manager. This was a theological magazine, with book reviews and thoughtful articles by leading theologians in the United States, Canada, and Europe. It also carried a limited amount of Seminary news. The editorials of Dr. de Blois were fascinating and illuminating. The retirement of Dr. de Blois, the continued financial depression, and the lack of interest in circulating the magazine forced the trustees, in 1941, to discontinue its publication. In the place of the *Christian Review* there was published the *Easterner,* a monthly paper (excepting July and August), which carried all the important news of the Seminary.

Quite a number of books were written by the professors during the presidency of Dr. de Blois. These helped to publicize the Seminary. The president himself wrote the following books: *Some Problems of the Modern Minister; John Bunyan, the Man; Fighters for Freedom; Evangelism in the*

New Age; and *The Church of Today—and Tomorrow.* Dr. B. C. Taylor wrote *Notes on the Old Testament.* Dr. J. B. Champion wrote *The Virgin Birth; Living Atonement;* and *More Than Atonement.* Dr. A. E. Harris wrote *Bible Books Outlined* and *The Psalms Outlined.* Dr. de Blois edited two books written by the professors, entitled *The Evangelical Faith* and *Christian Religious Education.* The last named was not published until 1939, but it was in process of preparation before Dr. de Blois retired. The *Bulletins,* the *Christian Review,* the *Easterner,* the books, the visits to the colleges and universities, and the advertising in newspapers and magazines gave Eastern considerable publicity during the first eleven years and helped to make her known as one of the outstanding theological seminaries in the North.

PUBLIC RELATIONS

Closely connected with the matter of publicity is the field of public relations. The term "public relations" was little used in the days of Eastern's beginning. The Seminary had received several substantial gifts, but the school was growing so fast that the trustees could not keep up with the constant demands that were made for new buildings, new professors, and new equipment. In October, 1927, the trustees engaged Dr. A. C. Hagaman of Minnesota as the Seminary's first financial agent. During the year he was with the school he gathered a long list of names and carried on a wide correspondence, but unfortunately he failed to raise any large amount of money. In the process, however, Eastern became much more widely known. After he left, there was no financial agent or field representative until 1943, when Rev. P. Vanis Slawter was appointed to that position.

MATERIAL AND SOCIAL PROGRESS

When Dr. de Blois became president in 1926, Eastern owned two buildings on South Rittenhouse Square. When he resigned in 1936, it owned seven buildings, six on Rittenhouse Square, and one on Spruce Street adjacent to the other buildings. The trustees thought they had land enough on which to erect a modern seminary building adequate to care for all future needs. To feed the resident students presented quite a problem. As is often the case, there was some dissatisfaction. In 1929 the students were requested by the president to appoint a committee which would assume the responsibility of operating the dining room. At first the students refused, feeling that their lack of knowledge and experience would militate against their success. After several months of negotiations, however, they agreed to try the experiment. A steward, an assistant steward, and a cook were employed. Students were told that all who were granted free rooms in the building must eat in the Seminary dining room.

After the students took over the operation of the dining room, complaints were seldom heard. The trustees accepted and approved the arrangement and offered to subsidize the expense of the dining room committee if any deficit existed at the end of the school year. So successful have been the efforts of the students that after thirty years this same plan, with but few changes, is still used.

In an institution of higher learning, the social needs of the students require considerable care. The crowded conditions of those early days, and the fact that the professors lived at a considerable distance from the school, made it difficult to develop an adequate social life at the Seminary; yet some degree of social fellowship, organized and supervised, was necessary. At first only a few socials were planned by the students. As time passed these socials became more numerous and better organized. On the whole, the spirit of the faculty and students was excellent.

The women needed some social life of their own. The wives of the professors and of the married students formed an organization for social and educational purposes which they called Hypatia. More recently the name of this organization has been changed to Alethenai.

Organizations were formed in each department of the Seminary to meet the needs of the students. When Dr. de Blois resigned the presidency, the following organizations existed: the Student's Association, the Evangelistic Association, the Dining Club, the Forensic Society, the League of Evangelical Students, the Homiletic Society, and Hypatia. Under their leadership the social, intellectual, disciplinary, and spiritual needs of the students were well cared for.

SUPERINTENDENTS

Dr. Walter R. Feser, a graduate of Eastern, was the very efficient superintendent of the buildings at Rittenhouse Square. In 1936 he resigned to accept a pastorate in Maine. Joseph W. Hill, the assistant treasurer, was elected to take Dr. Feser's place.

This brings to an end the story of Eastern's progress under the leadership of Dr. Austen Kennedy de Blois. One can see by this brief résumé that his task had not been an easy one. He carried heavy burdens, but he had a glorious and fruitful ministry as president of Eastern. He would have continued longer as president but his health failed. Two years after his resignation he was asked by the trustees to write the history of Eastern Baptist Theological Seminary for the first ten years. This he graciously consented to do and published the book under the title of *The Making of Ministers.* It is a well written book of 280 pages.

APPRECIATION

Many expressions of appreciation were received by Dr. de Blois at the time of his retirement. We close this chapter with excerpts from the message sent to him by the board of trustees: "The board of trustees . . . hereby records its sincere appreciation of the faithful and efficient service rendered the Seminary during the past ten years, by our retiring president, Dr. Austen K. de Blois.

"When Dr. de Blois assumed his duties as president of our Seminary, Eastern was a mere infant—one year old. . . . Obviously, what we needed was leadership—scholarly, judicious, aggressive, spiritual. Such leadership Dr. de Blois has given.

"After ten years of faithful service he resigns from the presidency leaving the Seminary in excellent condition. . . . Largely through him our Seminary has risen to an honorable position in the scholastic world. Through his influence also we have become recognized in the denomination, not merely as a standard theological school, but as one of the leading seminaries in the country.

"His scholarly habits and attainments, his fine teaching ability, his strong conservative convictions, his vigorous and aggressive spirit, his far-reaching vision, his strong grasp of modern problems, his success as an author, his achievements as editor of the *Christian Review,* his splendid contacts with the colleges and with the denomination have qualified Dr. de Blois for the roll of honor, and have placed Eastern Seminary in his debt forever. . . ."

Dr. de Blois passed away August 9, 1945.

III

EXPANSION AND PROGRESS

by

GORDON H. BAKER

EASTERN HAS BEEN FORTUNATE in its choice of presidents. All of them have been thoroughly good men who have fully met the needs of the Seminary in their terms of office. President Ball was the promoter and organizer, whose leadership was instrumental in bringing Eastern into being. President de Blois was the scholar who raised the Seminary to a place of recognition and high standing in the Baptist denomination and in the public view.

Founded in the midst of theological conflict which was almost world-wide, Eastern now faced a new struggle. Not only theologians but people everywhere were politically, economically, and emotionally disturbed. The ship of state was sailing a rough sea. In such a situation the schools of higher education were caught in the swirling currents of that day. Eastern was no exception. It needed at this time a leader who was wise, cultured, and possessed of executive ability; a man loyal to the truth and deeply consecrated to Christ; a captain who could steer the ship safely through the boisterous theological waters.

On the Pacific Coast was a hard working and successful pastor, Dr. Gordon Palmer. He was the minister of the large First Baptist Church of Pomona, California. Other churches had sought his leadership, but he was happy and contented in his chosen work. Probably it never occurred to him that a new and growing theological seminary in the East would be calling him to become its third president. After much prayer that the Holy Spirit would guide the trustees in their choice of a new president, a call was extended to Dr. Palmer. Startled and stunned by the challenge, he did not decide at once. He prayed about the matter and then wrote that if the trustees and the faculty were unanimous in favor of his coming to Eastern and would pledge him their loyalty, he would consider it a call from God and accept the challenge. The call was given May 12, 1936; he accepted it and arrived in December.

PROGRESS UNDER THE THIRD PRESIDENT

Dr. Gordon Palmer

While it was a high honor to be chosen president of Eastern, a school with a brief but noble past and a promising future, few men have ever had a more difficult task committed to them. World War II and a period of depression took place during his presidency. The theological controversy in the churches was at its height. The expenses of the Seminary were constantly increasing while the income during the depression years diminished. Economies had to be practiced in many directions. New rights had to be obtained from the State Board of Education. New professors had to be secured; numerous changes made in the curriculum; new buildings purchased; accreditation sought; contentions and conflicts dealt with. Dr. Palmer tackled them in a buoyant, confident, and humble spirit, and Eastern Seminary in spite of difficulties made marvelous progress under his leadership. The fact that there was no long period between the retirement of Dr. de Blois and the coming of Dr. Palmer was greatly in his favor.

The new president immediately endeavored to acquaint himself with existing conditions at Eastern. Having gathered the principal data, he proceeded to execute some of his plans. The trustees and the faculty gave him excellent support.

Of major importance in any theological seminary is its faculty. No school of any kind can ever be greater than its teaching staff. Dr. Palmer inherited a strong, intelligent, and consecrated group of professors. Most of them had been on the faculty from the beginning. Of the fourteen on the teaching staff of the Seminary and Collegiate Division when he came to Eastern, only five remained when he retired. One resigned to become president of another seminary. One retired because of poor health. Three were taken by death. Two retired because they had reached the age limit. Two resigned to accept appointments in other schools.

It seems sufficiently important to record here some of these faculty changes. On November 27, 1935, Dr. Wilber T. Elmore, professor of Church History and Missions, died. In 1936 Dr. William A. Mueller was chosen by the trustees to take his place. In 1937 Dr. Harry Watson Barras died, leaving vacant the chair of Homiletics. The president and trustees wanted to secure an outstanding preacher to fill this important position. Dr. J. C. Massee, retired from the pastorate of Tremont Temple, Boston, one of America's great preachers, was asked to teach this course temporarily. He taught with great effectiveness for a year and a half. Following Dr. Massee in 1941, Dr. W. H. Wrighton, of the Department of Philosophy of the University of Georgia, was called to fill the chair of Homiletics. Dr. Wrighton was really called to Eastern to fill the chair of English Bible; but since Dr. Maxwell had not yet retired, he was given the chair of Homiletics *ad interim*. In 1943 he was elected to the chair of English Bible. One year later, 1944, Dr. Wrighton resigned, and Dr. Clarence S. Roddy, pastor of the Baptist Temple in Brooklyn, New York, was called in his place.

The trustees elected Dr. Palmer to teach Homiletics with the understanding that he would have the right to engage any help he might need by way of special lecturers from the outside. But Dr. Palmer soon found he was too busy to carry this load.

Dr. Barnard C. Taylor passed away in 1937, leaving vacant the chair of Old Testament Interpretation and Hebrew. His successor was Professor W. E. Griffiths, who developed into one of our great teachers. Professor David Lee Jamison retired in 1941, and Culbert G. Rutenber succeeded him in the chair of Philosophy of Religion. Though young at the time of his election, he was a competent scholar and a superb teacher. Dr. J. B. Champion resigned in 1941, leaving vacant one of the most important chairs in the Seminary, that of Theology. We were fortunate to secure as his successor, Dr. William E. Powers, from the Northern Baptist Theological Seminary in Chicago. Here was a man of experience and unusual ability. Students who entered his classroom soon knew they were with a master in his field. Through the years Dr. Powers has helped his students to develop a theology which is both true to historic Christianity and relevant to the needs of the twentieth century.

Dr. Benjamin T. Livingston, who followed Dr. H. F. Stilwell in the chair of Evangelism and was largely responsible for the school's vigorous growth in evangelistic concern and endeavor, unfortunately was forced to resign because of ill health in the fall of 1941. He was succeeded for one year by Dr. W. H. Wrighton and then by Professor Albert G. Williams. Dr. Williams was called as professor of Evangelism and director of Placement and Practical Work. In the autumn of 1941, Dr. Donald Gorham resigned as head of the School of Christian Education, to take effect at the end of the school year, in May, 1942. His place was not filled immediately. Professor Joseph R. Bowman took care of the Christian education courses, along with his teaching of music, and Dr. Carl H. Morgan carried the work during 1945-46. In 1946, Dr. C. Adrian Heaton was called from the Northern Baptist Theological Seminary in Chicago to become head of the School of Christian Education at Eastern. With the able assistance of his wife, Ada Beth Heaton, he built up this school into one of the best of its kind in America.

Professor William A. Mueller resigned the chair of Church History at Eastern in 1943 to accept a similar position at Colgate Rochester Divinity School. Professor Robert G. Torbet, his very able and efficient assistant, was elected to take his place. A number of important additions were made to the collegiate faculty. In 1944, Paul B. Cooly was called to the chair of English Language and Literature. Dr. Evan A. Reiff of Atchison, Kansas, succeeded him one year later. Dr. Alexander Grigolia was called from Wheaton College, Wheaton, Illinois, to teach Anthropology. In 1945, Dr. Samuel M. Ortegon of California was called to become professor of Sociology and Spanish; and Dr. W. W. Adams resigned as professor of New Testament Interpretation and Greek to become president of Central Baptist Theological Seminary, Kansas City, Kansas, Dr. Carl H. Morgan was elected to succeed Dr. Adams. That same year, Dr. Willis E. Elliott was chosen as professor of Greek and Hebrew, and remained with Eastern for four years. He resigned to continue his studies.

These are most of the changes which took place in the faculty while Dr. Palmer was president. That Dr. Palmer held deep convictions regarding the calling of men to the faculty may be seen from one of his reports to the trustees in which he said: "I believe men should be called to teach at Eastern just as truly as men are called to be pastors. God has His men in preparation for openings here. It is for us to discern His will and follow His guidance. I make an earnest request that you remember us in your prayers that we may be guided to the right men to fill the vacancies on our teaching staff."

In selecting new teachers Dr. Palmer was unusually cautious to be sure that the trustees were obtaining the kind of men who would be a real asset to the school in spirit, ability, and theological soundness.

The second problem the president had to face was the theological controversy among Northern Baptists. Eastern was started as a conservative theological seminary, loyal to the Baptist denomination (which at that time was the Northern Baptist Convention), its official agencies, and its missionary and educational institutions. What attitude should the Seminary take now that several major groups had separated themselves from the Northern Baptist Convention and formed conventions of their own? Naturally, they expected that Eastern would pull out of the Northern Baptist Convention with them. But Eastern took no such step, for it believed that at least eighty-five per cent of those who remained in the Northern Baptist Convention also were conservative. The fact that a small group pulled out and used the name "Conservative" did not alter this situation. Eastern took its stand with the great body of conservative Baptists who remained loyal to the Convention and its agencies.

The two major groups that had withdrawn from the Northern Baptist Convention and formed new conventions became known as the General Association of Regular Baptists (G.A.R.B.) and the Conservative Baptist Association (C.B.A.). The peace of the Seminary was considerably disturbed because representatives of these groups became propagandists within the school and worked for their cause. The trustees eventually found that they had to make an important decision. So long as these various groups were free to work from within, there would be contention and confusion in the Seminary. It appeared to many that the aim of the so-called "conservative" group was to take over Eastern for themselves. If such was their aim, they failed in their efforts. The trustees took the position that the main business of Eastern is to train men and women for the gospel ministry, no matter where they might serve. They also decided to continue to work within the framework of the Northern Baptist Convention and its official agencies.

Let us turn now to the problem of buildings. Even though Eastern owned six buildings on Rittenhouse Square and one on Spruce Street, and intended to erect a modern seminary building on that location, the plan failed because of the zoning laws. For this reason and for the further fact that the building being used had been declared unsafe, it became necessary to look elsewhere for a new property. The trustees prayed for months about this matter and then made an offer to the Penn Athletic Club for the purchase of their building. Eastern could not afford the price that was asked, however, so they were compelled to drop that project and look elsewhere. It was suggested that they might investigate the possibility of purchasing the Green Hill Farms Hotel, a private hotel located at City Line and Lancaster Avenue. Negotiations were begun with the owners at once, with the result that in May, 1939, the trustees purchased the Green Hill Farms Hotel, with all its furnishings, for the sum of $650,000. This was a great bargain. It furnished rooms enough for all single students, and gave the school room to expand. In December, 1945, the trustees purchased the Wynnewood Apartments, one block away for $210,000, to be used as housekeeping apartments for married students with children. This magnificent four-story building, constructed of brick and stone and containing fifty-six apartments, was named Eastern Hall. Later the trustees purchased the vacant lot on the corner, next to Eastern Hall, as a playground for the children of the students, and also to prevent it from being used for some undesirable purpose.

Eastern needed a building for its professors, many of whom had to live miles from the Seminary to get suitable accommodations. In October, 1946, the Lancaster Apartments, 6351-6355 Lancaster Avenue, were purchased for $102,000.

Eastern suffered a great loss in the death of Ralph I. Levering, April 30, 1943. Mr. Levering had been chairman of the finance committee from the founding of the Seminary. At the annual meeting of the trustees in May, 1934, he was called from his position in the West Philadelphia Title and Trust Company to become treasurer of Eastern Seminary, at considerably less salary than he was getting at the bank. As treasurer he would have to care for all mortgages, stocks and bonds, and handle all the finances at Eastern. Few people will ever know what Mr. Levering meant to Eastern. It was through his sane advice that the large gifts received by Eastern in those early days were wisely invested, and the financial interests of Eastern safely guarded. Upon the death of Mr. Levering, the trustees elected Dr. Harvey Bartle to fill the office of treasurer. It might be well to quote here Dr. Bartle's eulogy of Mr. Levering:

> "We shall miss Ralph I. Levering, whose devotion to, knowledge of, and concern for the best interest of Eastern Seminary have been an inspiration to all with whom he has been associated in the work since its inception. He had a wealth of details at his command, an intuitive financial sense, reliable judgment, a noble and sympathetic Christian attitude which fitted him admirably for the position and place he occupied in the activities of the Seminary, which he loved. He distinguished himself honorably, courageously, and effectively."

The financial pressure during the long depression and the period of the Second World War was tremendous. In five weeks, in 1941, Eastern's investments suffered a depreciation in value of $151,320. War conditions worked havoc in the stock market, and Eastern had large holdings, with the result that the financial losses combined with increasing expenses put Eastern under a strain. Fortunately the trustees had a substantial reserve fund of over $70,000, but that was fast slipping away. They cut expenses wherever possible and in a few years they were in a stronger position. Dr. Palmer's advice during this period was very helpful to the trustees. The work of trying to pilot a school like Eastern through such troubled waters was not easy.

Eastern needed two more new buildings: a chapel and a library. To raise funds for the erection of these buildings, a campaign was inaugurated in connection with the twentieth anniversary of the founding of the Seminary. In September, 1943, Rev. P. Vanis Slawter was called to be field representative. He visited the churches, secured gifts for the Seminary, and persuaded many churches to include Eastern in their annual budgets. Mr. Slawter gave an excellent account of his stewardship. He did faithful and efficient work and obtained good results.

One of the problems in a school like Eastern is adequate aid for students. Occasionally a young man will leave his business and come to the Seminary with a nest-egg of his own. This, however, is the exception. Most theological students are poor and need help. Eastern has never tried to "buy" students, but it has tried to help them. Scholarships have been created for that purpose. In this way the Seminary has been able to encourage students, who, but for this help, would have been tempted to quit their studies or go to some other institution. Dr. Palmer did much to encourage the development of this plan. Indeed, he contributed all his honoraria to a fund for helping needy students.

The *Christian Review,* which Dr. de Blois had edited so efficiently for more than ten years, ceased publication in 1941. This was not according to Dr. Palmer's desire, but since the cost was very great and the circulation limited, it was felt that a smaller paper containing more Seminary news would be preferable. This new publication was called *The Easterner.*

The library at Eastern continued to grow. The number of annual accessions soon taxed existing facilities and need for additional space became imperative.

In 1938, Miss Eleanor Price resigned as librarian, and her assistant, Miss Josephine B. Carson, was elected to succeed her, with Miss Margaret Tucker, a student at Eastern, as her assistant. In 1946, Mr. W. J. Hand was elected librarian, while he continued to teach in the field of science. In 1947, Eastern's library became a member of the American Theological Library Association, the American Library Association, and the Special Library Association. That same year

Eastern's library was listed in the Union Library Catalogue, which vastly increased its effectiveness. At this time the library contained approximately 26,000 volumes.

While Dr. Palmer was greatly interested in lifting the level of scholarship at Eastern, he was equally concerned that the Seminary retain its sound evangelical point of view and deep spiritual commitment. In 1941, Dr. Palmer said: "I believe we are moving toward more effective services, deeper spirituality, higher scholarship, and withal greater accomplishments for our Lord through Eastern. So far as I know there is no deviation from our basic statement of faith."

The trustees did not wait until the end to express their appreciation of Dr. Palmer's services and leadership. In 1942, the trustees passed the following resolution: "That the board of trustees of The Eastern Baptist Theological Seminary hereby express its profound appreciation of the excellent services rendered by our president during the past year. We feel that we have in Dr. Palmer a true man of God, who has given lavishly of his splendid strength and ability to further the best interests of our Seminary, and we pledge him anew our loyalty and support." This same attitude of confidence and trust by the trustees was sustained in Dr. Palmer to the day of his resignation.

On another occasion Dr. Palmer wrote to the trustees his own sentiments. He said: "Kindly accept my heartiest appreciation for the wholehearted and united support which has come to me through the board of trustees. You have always encouraged me in the work and your confidence and faith are a challenge to me to give my utmost and my best. The task is so great, the responsibilities so many, and the obligations so heavy that I often feel completely unequal to the demands, but God knows that we are serving, not for credit in the eyes of man, but that we might have a good conscience void of offence toward God and man and that we might have the Father's divine approval." This expresses better than anything one could say, the spirit of Eastern's third president.

Dr. Palmer sought to secure for Eastern the right to grant the bachelor of arts degree by expanding the pretheological courses to four years and so correlating them with the theological training that in six years a young man might receive the bachelor of arts and the bachelor of theology degrees. The goal was reached in 1938 when the State Board of Education in Pennsylvania granted that right. For six years of study the student received the bachelor of arts and the bachelor of divinity degrees.

Another goal sought by Dr. Palmer was the establishment of a retirement plan to provide old-age security for the faculty and staff. First steps toward his goal were taken in 1947. The strengthening of the faculty, the deepening of the spiritual life of the students, the securing of new and adequate buildings, the endowing of the chair of Missions, the establishing of additional scholarships, the fostering of the missionary spirit in the Seminary, the kindling of the evangelistic flame among students and faculty, the developing of the library, and the maintaining of a wholesome esprit de corps in the community life of the Seminary—these were some of the goals Dr. Palmer sought to attain.

On March 16, 1948, Dr. Palmer resigned the presidency after twelve years of strenuous service and wise leadership. To express their appreciation of him, the board of trustees named the main building "Gordon Palmer Hall." But the greatest tribute to his superb leadership is to be found in the hundreds of young men and women, trained at Eastern during his presidency, who have gone to all parts of the world to preach and teach the glorious gospel of Christ.

PROGRESS UNDER THE FOURTH PRESIDENT

Dr. Gilbert Lee Guffin

For more than a year after Dr. Palmer resigned, Eastern was without a president. The administration was placed in the hands of a steering committee of which Dean Carl H. Morgan and Dr. Harvey Bartle were cochairmen. Dr. Morgan was in charge of the educational and spiritual program, and Dr. Bartle cared for the finances and the equipment. A special committee was appointed to look for and recommend a new president. Recognizing the great importance of this position, the board again prayed earnestly that the Holy Spirit might guide them in making their choice.

Among the many names suggested was that of Dr. Gilbert L. Guffin, a graduate of Eastern in the class of 1935. He was young, cultured, well-trained, and successful in everything he attempted to do. Having graduated from Mercer University in 1930, and from Eastern Seminary in 1935, from which he received the B.D. degree, he returned to Eastern as a graduate student and later received from Eastern the Th.M. and Th.D. degrees. He had been elected to the board of trustees of Eastern on May 26, 1941. At that time he was pastor of the First Baptist Church at Merchantville, New Jersey. From Merchantville he was called to the First Baptist Church, Jasper, Alabama, where he rendered conspicuous service. The authorities at Howard College recognized his ability and called him to be the founder and first director of their Extension Division for Christian Training, a program since known as the Howard Plan and widely used now in the South and in some areas of the North. He had become widely known through this extension program.

After several conferences with the board, Dr. Guffin received a unanimous call to become the fourth president of The Eastern Baptist Theological Seminary.

When Dr. Guffin became president of Eastern, he faced many unusual problems. The process of growth itself multiplied his responsibilities and added to his administrative burdens. One of the first tasks to confront the new president was the securing of full accreditation by the American Association of Theological Schools, of which it was an associate member. Every year the lack of it had made it more difficult to attract promising students. Dr. Palmer had wrestled with this problem during most of his presidency, but the presence of the Collegiate Department always proved to be a stumbling block. The time had now come, however, when some definite action had to be taken or both the Seminary and the College, it was feared, would suffer serious loss.

The Middle States Association of Colleges and Secondary Schools and the American Association of Theological Schools had both declared that Eastern could not be accredited while the College Department was attached to it, though the former later modified this position. The trustees concluded that they would have to close the College Department or find a new campus and a larger faculty and separate the two schools. There was no disposition on the part of the trustees to close the College Department; on the other hand, they did not see how they could finance a new campus and a separate school. However, since the Seminary was started by faith, for it had no money in the beginning, the trustees decided again to move by faith.

Early in 1951 word came to the trustees that the Walton Estate, known as Walmarthon, in St. Davids, eight miles from the Seminary, consisting of forty-five acres of beautiful rolling, wooded, and landscaped ground, with several buildings, would soon be on the market. The trustees examined the property carefully, purchased it, and after some rebuilding, it has become a truly magnificent college campus. Eastern Baptist College was incorporated on July 11, 1952. This action cleared the way for regional accreditation.

On May 3, 1954 both the Seminary and the College were accredited by the Middle States Association of Colleges and Secondary Schools; and later in the same year the Seminary was accredited by the American Association of Theological Schools.

The story of the College and its progress is a fascinating one but cannot be told here. This much should be said, however, that while there are two boards of trustees, separately elected by each school, they are the same persons, and the president of the Seminary is also the president of the College. The College now has a campus of eighty-one acres and fifteen buildings, including a new gymnasium. It has a faculty of twenty-seven professors and four instructors. In these developments Dr. Guffin has led with determination, calmness, and skill.

One day, early in 1950, the executive committee was meeting in Philadelphia, when it was announced that Mrs. Laws had brought with her Mrs. Marguerite T. Doane, who wanted to speak to the trustees. She was admitted to the meeting and said that she wanted to give to The Eastern Baptist Theological Seminary a building in memory of Dr. Curtis Lee Laws, who had been a friend of the family for many years. She wanted to know what building was most needed. The trustees pointed out that they needed a library building and a new chapel, and they further pointed out that they would cost about the same amount of money. At a later date, Mrs.

Doane reported that she would give the memorial chapel at an estimated cost of $325,000. When the chapel was finished, the cost, with the furnishings, actually came to $413,-000. This was a great and munificent gift. Since its dedication in 1951, the memorial chapel has come to play a large part in the life of the Seminary.

The lower floor of the building was dedicated to the memory of William Howard Doane, father of the donor, greatly beloved for his many beautiful hymns. When the chapel was completed, a $25,000 pipe organ was installed. This organ was a gift of Mrs. A. Otis Birch of California in memory of her mother, and it had come to the Seminary while Dr. Palmer was president. Only part of it had been used in the old chapel. The new chapel seats 650 people and, when school is in session, it is used practically every day.

Another significant achievement was the erection of the new library and classroom building for the Seminary at a cost of approximately $260,000. This building was made possible by the gifts of many individuals and churches, as part of the 30th Anniversary Development Program. It is a well constructed and commodious building connecting Gordon Palmer Hall and the old classroom and library structure. In this building the Austen K. de Blois Memorial Library is located together with the reading room, files, and librarian's work space. The classrooms are large and well adapted to the needs of graduate students. These two buildings—the new library building and the new chapel—add much to the strength, beauty, and convenience of the campus.

Faculty changes are inevitable in every fast growing school. When Dr. Guffin came to Eastern as president, the College was still a part of the Seminary, and the two faculties were, in part, combined. Dr. Lyle Bristol was chosen as dean of the college in 1951. In 1949 George S. Claghorn was engaged to teach in the College Department. He received his Ph.D. degree from the University of Pennsylvania, and in 1954, upon the resignation of Dr. Bristol, became Dean of the College.

On September 11, 1949, Dr. J. H. Telford, professor of Missions, died, leaving vacant this important chair. In the fall of 1950, Dr. Theodore E. Bubeck, a missionary from Africa, was engaged to teach during a furlough period. Following him, Dr. H. C. Jackson of Kansas City, Kansas, was called to head the Missionary Department. Professor Jackson accepted a call to the Southern Baptist Theological Seminary in the fall of 1954, and Dr. Walter Bruce Davis, an alumnus of Eastern, and former missionary in East Pakistan, was invited to occupy the chair of Missions as a guest teacher. So well did Dr. Davis perform his task that in March, 1955, he was elected a full professor of Missions. In addition to his duties as teacher, he is also the greatly-beloved chaplain of the Seminary.

In January, 1950, Dr. Evan A. Reiff resigned the chair of English to accept the position of president of Sioux Falls College. Mrs. Orpha Kutnow was chosen as instructor and acting supervisor in the English department. In the spring of 1950, Professor J. Wesley Ingles of Bates College, Maine, was called to be head of the English Department. Dr. Ingles is an able teacher, scholar, and author. Professor Robert Proctor was chosen as instructor in Psychology, and Dr. Robert C. Campbell, now dean of the California Baptist Theological Seminary, was engaged as a full-time instructor in the College Division.

At the close of the school year of 1950-1951, Dr. Clarence S. Roddy resigned to accept a teaching position in another school. The trustees sought to replace him with the best man they could find. Dr. Nelson Baker, of the faculty of the California Baptist Theological Seminary, a graduate of Eastern, was engaged as Dr. Roddy's successor. Dr. Baker is proving himself to be a very worthy scholar and teacher.

Professor W. E. Griffiths resigned from the chair of Old Testament Interpretation and Hebrew (1952) to accept the pastorate of the First Baptist Church, Norristown, Pennsylvania, and Dr. Edward R. Dalglish, of the faculty of Gordon Divinity School, Boston, Massachusetts, was engaged to take his place. In this case, as in others, Eastern gave up a good man and received another good man in return. Dr. Dalglish is an able scholar and a skillful teacher in a very demanding field.

Professor Robert G. Torbet was outstanding as professor of Church History at Eastern. He received his Ph.D. degree at the University of Pennsylvania, and while he was teaching at Eastern he wrote his book entitled, *A History of the Baptists.* When he resigned to go with the Board of Education and Publication of the American Baptist Convention, the trustees selected Professor Norman H. Maring to replace him. Professor Maring also has a Ph.D., received from the University of Maryland. He is scholarly and gifted. He is an excellent teacher, and greatly respected by professors, students, and Baptist historians generally.

The School of Christian Education is an important branch of the work at Eastern Seminary. In 1947, Professor C. Adrian Heaton was called from the Northern Baptist Theological Seminary in Chicago to be head of this school. In 1950, his wife, Ada Beth Heaton, Ph.D., was engaged to serve with him. At that time she was teaching in the School of Education of Temple University. Through their efforts the School of Christian Education has become one of the best in the land. In the fall of 1953, Professor Heaton was elected president of the American Association of Schools of Religious Education. This Association accredited Eastern's School of Christian Education in 1951, three years before the Seminary was accredited by the Middle States Association of Colleges and Secondary Schools and the American Association of Theological Schools. Dr. Heaton had been sought for a number of years by other schools, but had chosen to remain at Eastern. In the summer of 1959, the presidency of the California Baptist Theological Seminary became vacant and Dr. Heaton was persuaded to accept that important post. He began his work there in December, 1959.

Dr. Norman W. Paullin, pastor of the Grace Baptist Temple, Philadelphia, was requested to give part of his time to the teaching of Homiletics at Eastern. He began doing so in the fall of 1951. Dr. Andrew W. Blackwood, retired from Princeton, also was engaged as a guest teacher. In 1954, Dr. Paullin was elected a full-time professor in the chair of Homiletics. For many years he had been recognized as a great preacher and had been in constant demand for public addresses. In 1957, he was elected vice-president of the American Baptist Convention where he served with distinction. Recently arrangements were made by which Dr. Paullin and Dr. Williams exchanged positions. Dr. Williams now teaches Homiletics and Dr. Paullin occupies the chair of Evangelism and Pastoral Ministry.

One of the bright spots in Eastern's story is the coming of Dr. Arthur B. Crabtree as professor of Theology. Dr. Crabtree is a graduate of the University of Manchester, England, and of the Baptist Theological Seminary, Manchester. He has a Th.D. degree from the University of Zurich. He is a theologian of great ability and growing reputation. He is a man of deep consecration and a magnetic preacher.

Among those who have contributed mightily to the growth

and influence of Eastern, the name of Culbert G. Rutenber stands high. From his earliest years as a student at Eastern he attracted the attention of his teachers as one having the rare combination of a brilliant mind and a humble spirit. His passion for men touched all areas of life. As a teacher at Eastern for nearly twenty years, he guided the students magnificently not only into the profundities of the philosophy of religion, but also into the broad areas of the life and practice of the Christian faith.

Through most of his years at Eastern he was much sought after by other schools. Ultimately he felt led to accept the invitation of Andover Newton Theological School, and it was with regret that it became necessary to accept his resignation in the fall of 1958. In the summer of 1959, the trustees called Dr. Thorwald W. Bender, of the Northern Baptist Theological Seminary in Chicago, to become professor of Philosophy of Religion and Theology. Dr. Bender has made a most favorable impression on the faculty and the students. He will certainly make a large place for himself here and in our Baptist family.

The Graduate School still continues to operate and now grants the Th.M. degree. The doctor's degree, suspended a few years ago, has not yet been restored; but consideration is now being given to the restoration of this program. Each autumn the faculty has a helpful retreat. During the school year there are such extra-curricular events as a spiritual vision week, evangelistic conferences, missionary programs, rural emphasis week, daily chapel services, prayer meetings for the faculty, and prayer meetings for the students, in addition to the regular academic program. During June and July Eastern provides three two-week terms of elective Seminary courses in the Summer School.

Eastern has a magnificent building for married students

with children, but until recently it had no housekeeping facilities for married students without children. These couples lived in Gordon Palmer Hall and ate in the dining room, or in some cases they rented rooms away from the campus. To overcome this deficiency, at least in part, twelve apartments were developed during the past year in Gordon Palmer Hall. These are for students without children, where they may do housekeeping.

Perhaps the greatest expansion under Dr. Guffin's leadership is to be seen in the Public Relations Department. As the Seminary grew and expanded its program, more financial help was needed for operating expenses. On November 6, 1951, Rev. P. Vanis Slawter resigned as field secretary to accept the pastorate of the Blockley Baptist Church, Philadelphia. It was decided to venture on a larger promotional program. Mr. Harry J. Albus, a man of wide experience in promotional work, was engaged as field and promotional representative. Mr. Albus did excellent work, but still there was need of greater expansion in Eastern's promotional program. Mr. Albus remained about two years and then resigned. The trustees chose Mr. John A. Baird, Jr., one of their own number, to be the president's assistant and general director of the Public Relations Department. Mr. Baird was given a full staff to assist him in this department and to enable the school to make more contacts with the churches and the public.

A financial campaign is conducted annually to help meet the growing needs of the school. In 1955, the thirtieth anniversary of Eastern Seminary, an organized effort was made to raise a special development fund of $350,000. A committee was formed of which Dr. Earl V. Pierce of Minneapolis was the honorary chairman, Dr. Charles S. Walton, Jr., general chairman, and Paul E. Almquist, national gifts chairman. This campaign ran for a little over a year and in May, 1957, it was reported that the goal had been reached. Despite this constant growth Eastern was determined to make further progress. In 1956, it was decided to appoint a survey committee to study the future needs of the school and to suggest how its work could be made more effective. A strong committee under the chairmanship of Mr. Frank F. Middleswart gave thorough study to the whole structure and immediate future of the school. It investigated such items as: curriculum, public relations, in-service training, recruitment of students, placement of graduates, placement of alumni, administration and organization, business management, physical facilities, student life, and the denominational relationships of the school. After three years of study the committee presented a seventeen page report containing important suggestions for future growth. Implementation of this plan is now in progress.

When the Institutional Budget was adopted by the American Baptist Convention, all of the Baptist seminaries were asked to participate in it officially. Eastern hesitated to join the plan because of its widely scattered alumni constituency and the restrictions which the Institutional Budget at first seemed to impose. However, in the spring of 1959, the trustees decided to enter the Institutional Budget and made application to the Board of Education and Publication of the American Baptist Convention for recognition. Applications were made also to the State Conventions of Pennsylvania, New Jersey, New York, District of Columbia, West Virginia, and Delaware for special recognition. Other states may be solicited for similar consideration. Henceforth any church in the denomination may contribute to Eastern through the Institutional Budget and receive credit for it in the denominational funds.

Another important promotional development of recent

I. Levering, and Rev. P. Vanis Slawter have already been named in these chapters. Several others should be mentioned here.

CURTIS LEE LAWS

Dr. Curtis Lee Laws was a charter trustee of Eastern. He was keenly interested from the beginning in Eastern's spiritual, educational, and material progress. He attended the meetings regularly for twenty years and his counsel was always helpful. Through his personal influence, and through the *Watchman-Examiner,* a paper which he owned and edited, he made many friends for Eastern Seminary. It was through his influence that Miss Mary Colgate of Yonkers, New York, placed Eastern in her will for $250,000. Many other substantial gifts came to Eastern from and through Dr. Laws. He served on the executive and instruction committees for all of the twenty years he was a trustee. He had a rare sense of humor and was a delightful conversationalist. His worth to Eastern will never be adequately evaluated.

MRS. SUSAN T. LAWS

When Dr. Laws died, July 7, 1946, Mrs. Laws was elected a member of the board of trustees. She was a quiet soul but was always thinking of ways to help Eastern. She too, like her late husband, was constantly seeking to secure gifts for the Seminary. Her simple act of visiting Mrs. Marguerite T. Doane was partly responsible for the gift of the new chapel. Much could be said of the effective services rendered to Eastern by this quiet little woman, but the tribute offered by her fellow trustees when she resigned because of ill-health is worth recording here.

"Inasmuch as Mrs. Susan T. Laws has served with distinction as a trustee of The Eastern Baptist Theological Seminary and Eastern Baptist College and has brought to the work of the instruction and executive committees, and other committees, intelligent understanding and discerning leadership, and inasmuch as she has carried on in the noble tradition of her late husband, Dr. Curtis Lee Laws, one of the founders of Eastern, and has been used as a liaison between our school and potential donors, such as Marguerite T. Doane, whose generous gift made possible the Curtis Lee Laws memorial chapel and the William Howard Doane hall of sacred music, and inasmuch as Mrs. Laws has given so generously of her time, talent, and substance in the interest of Eastern, BE IT RESOLVED, that the executive committee of our board of trustees express its deep appreciation for Mrs. Laws' lasting contribution to the work of Eastern and to the kingdom of God. . . ."

M. JOSEPH TWOMEY

Dr. Twomey was elected to the board of trustees on May 17, 1937, and served with distinction until the time of his death, October 29, 1948. At the time of his election he was pastor of the Grace Baptist Temple in Philadelphia. He was a man of far-reaching vision and penetrating insights, with a faculty for reaching sane conclusions. While others were discussing details, Dr. Twomey often was writing out resolutions; usually they were adopted. His opinions were always highly valued.

JOHN A. HAINER

Dr. Hainer was pastor of the Blockley Baptist Church, Philadelphia, and a charter trustee of Eastern. Few men were more gracious than Dr. Hainer. He had a lovable disposition and a kindly manner that won him a host of friends. He served as secretary of the board of trustees for fifteen years until he passed away in April, 1941. He was quiet and unassuming, but an indefatigable worker and a successful pastor. He loved Eastern and spent a large portion of his time helping it grow. When he passed away, his gracious wife became the house-mother at Eastern Seminary. Her presence was a benediction to the administration, the faculty, and the students.

HARVEY BARTLE, M.D.

Dr. Bartle became a trustee of Eastern in 1942. At that time he was medical director of the Pennsylvania Railroad system. For a number of years he was a member of the finance committee, and on the death of the treasurer, Ralph I. Levering, April 30, 1943, he was elected treasurer of the board of trustees of Eastern Seminary. In that office he has served with efficiency and fidelity. He carries his heavy responsibilities gladly as a service to the Lord. In addition to his position as treasurer, he is chairman of the finance committee. Eastern is greatly indebted to its treasurer for the faithful and devoted services he has rendered.

HARRY L. JENKINS

Mr. Jenkins is a Philadelphia lawyer, a member of Grace Baptist Temple, where he has taught an adult Bible class for many years. He is a leader among the Baptist forces of Philadelphia and the State of Pennsylvania, having served as president of the Pennsylvania Baptist Convention. He was elected a trustee in May, 1943. His legal knowledge has been invaluable to the trustees. He is a member of the executive committee, the building committee, the finance committee, the trustees-faculty committee, and chairman of the nominating committee. Mr. Jenkins has helped the Seminary greatly with his valuable legal knowledge and advice.

CHARLES S. WALTON, JR.

Charles S. Walton, Jr., deserves to have a book written about him. He will doubtless be mentioned by others in this volume, but I cannot refrain from referring to him in this survey. What survey could be just and omit mention of the name of the man who seems to be the soul of Eastern? Mr. Walton has been chairman of the board of trustees since 1939, chairman of the executive committee, and chairman of the building committee, for both the Seminary and the College. Few men have given so much time, thought, and money to Eastern as has Mr. Walton. He is one of God's good men. Since he has retired from business, he has given even more time to Eastern than in former years. In May, 1959, Eastern Baptist College conferred on him the LL.D. degree as a partial recognition of its great debt to this noble man of God.

PAUL E. ALMQUIST

Paul E. Almquist came to Philadelphia from Chicago, Illinois, as a representative of the Remington Rand Company. He was an active Christian worker before he came to Philadelphia and Eastern soon elected him to the board of trustees. He is vice-chairman of the board, chairman of the public relations committee, a member of the executive committee, and of the finance committee. His mental acumen, business experience, love for Eastern, strong Christian faith, and deep consecration make him one of the most valuable members of the board. Through his efforts the public relations committee is now the strongest it has ever been.

THORNLEY B. WOOD

Mr. Wood came on the board May 15, 1939, as a young businessman, full of consecrated enthusiasm. He is assistant secretary of the board of trustees, a member of the executive committee, of the building committee, of the finance committee, of the trustees-faculty committee, of the public relations committee, and chairman of the bequest committee. One characteristic of Mr. Wood, other than his enthusiasm, is his willingness to perform any task that is assigned to him. More than that, Mr. Wood has initiative and is full of original ideas. He is giving a great deal of time in the service of his Lord through Eastern. Mr. Wood was one of the original members of the board of trustees, serving until 1930. After an absence of nine years, he consented to return to the board and has served continuously since that date.

BENJAMIN P. BROWNE

No finer Christian gentleman could be found anywhere than Dr. Benjamin P. Browne. He is the executive director of the Division of Christian Publications of the Board of Education and Publication of the American Baptist Convention. In the interest of that board he frequently travels across the country and is well known among our Baptist people. He came on the board of Eastern in 1955, and he is one of its most helpful members. He serves on the executive committee, the instruction committee, the nominating committee, and was for some time chairman of the library and honorary degrees committees. He knows the Baptist denomination as few men do.

He is an indefatigable worker, a judicious advisor, and trusted leader.

OTHERS

Other trustees who should receive special mention are Mrs. Henry W. Peabody, W. Theodore Taylor, Clifford C. Meeden, C. Gordon Brownville, Frank Middleswart, Earl V. Pierce, Frank Brasington, Ralph L. Mayberry, John E. Briggs, William P. Haug. Each one of them, and many others, deserve fuller mention than is possible here. Dr. Mayberry and the writer are the only two persons living who were at the first meeting when the Eastern Seminary was organized. They have seen its progress through the years and rejoice in its hopeful outlook.

DR. GORDON H. BAKER

(The following is added to this chapter by the editor)

When Eastern's record is fully written, a large place will be given to the remarkable part Dr. Gordon H. Baker, himself a remarkable man, has had in it. He was one of the small group who, as elsewhere stated, took part in founding the Seminary. At that time he was already a leading pastor in the denomination, an author, and a man of wide influence. He could not have known then that although he was nearly fifty years old at the time, he would still be an active, vigorous participant in the work of the board thirty-five years later.

Many of the pivotal decisions made across the years resulted from Dr. Baker's insights and concerns. The record will disclose moreover that some of the most decisive, meaningful actions of the board resulted from motions made by Dr. Baker.

The devotion and dedication of Dr. Baker to Eastern have not been excelled by any one who has had a part on the board or otherwise in the work of the school. Dr. Baker has an almost unbroken record of attendance on board and committee meetings. His actual time spent in board work for the school would, if put together, add up to several full years. Even at eighty-three years of age, he still comes to Philadelphia with unabating regularity and promptness—sometimes as often as once per week over extended periods of time, and often for night meetings as well—to look after the interests of the school. He has served on most of the committees of the board and for years has been its faithful secretary.

Eastern owes an inestimable debt to Dr. Baker. His noble and generous contributions to this institution will continue to be an inspiration and challenge, as it has been in the past, to all who are connected with it.

IV

THIS WE BELIEVE

by

ARTHUR B. CRABTREE

THE OCCASION OF THE STATEMENT

CONFESSIONS OF FAITH are frequently, though not invariably, the fruit of controversy. The Nicene Creed, for instance, arose from the Arian controversy, and the various Protestant Confessions of Faith from the controversy of Protestants with Rome and their controversies among themselves.

Eastern's doctrinal statement, like the Confessions, is to some degree an outcome of controversy—the controversy which raged in the early decades of the present century between "liberals" or "modernists" on the one side and "conservatives" or "evangelicals" on the other.

Liberalism or modernism was essentially an attempt to adapt Christianity to the needs and ideas of the modern world. It took many forms. There was liberalism of a Hegelian type which minimized the distinction between God and man, which made Christ but a symbol of the divinity of all men, or which minimized the gravity of sin and the need for reconciliation. There was liberalism of a Kantian or Neo-

Kantian type which elevated the ethical at the expense of the ontological, elevated the love of God at the expense of his holiness (Ritschl), or which reduced Christianity to the affirmation of the Fatherhood of God, the brotherhood of man, and the infinite value of the human soul (Harnack). There was the liberalism of a naturalistic type which either eliminated God altogether or so identified him with the immanent evolutionary process that nothing was left of his transcendence. There was the liberalism of the Social Gospel, which sometimes became so obsessed with the sins of society that it forgot the sins of individuals. And there were all manner of combinations of these liberalisms. That there was something laudable in these attempts to preach the gospel in a modern way to modern men cannot be denied. Yet some things essential to the authentic apostolic gospel of the New Testament were lost in the process. The majesty, holiness, transcendence, and triunity of God, the gravity of sin, the uniqueness of Christ in his incarnation, vicarious death, resurrection, and return, were being obscured or denied, and it was felt that the time had come to reaffirm these forgotten factors.

This was the concern of the founding fathers of Eastern, and it finds expression in the first seven articles of the Statement. The second concern of the founding fathers was that Eastern should be a Baptist school, working loyally with Baptists without disrespect to other denominations. This finds expression in the last two articles.

THE CONTENT OF THE STATEMENT

What is the theological content of the Statement? In the exposition which follows, we shall take the liberty of transposing several articles for the sake of coherence.

We believe that the Bible, composed of the Old and New Testaments, is inspired of God, and is of supreme and final authority in faith and life.

In this article the Bible is placed in the center of theology and in the center of instruction. Not that tradition or science or philosophy is despised, but the Bible is made supreme. It is "inspired of God, and of supreme and final authority in faith and life."

Note that while the inspiration of the Scriptures is here plainly taught, no particular *theory* of inspiration is propounded, any more than a particular *theory* of inspiration is propounded in the Bible itself. All that is insisted upon is the fact of the inspiration of the Scriptures by the Spirit of God. We are left free to seek and adopt whatever *theory* of inspiration best accords with the nature and content of Scripture.

Along with the inspiration, the supremacy and the authority of Scripture are affirmed; supremacy, that is, over tradition and philosophy, and authority over the church and the Christian individual.

The supremacy of Scripture does not mean that the Bible is the sole source of theology. We may learn from tradition and we may learn from philosophy. But the Scripture remains the supreme source and the ultimate norm. All theological confessions, including Eastern's Statement, are subordinate to it.

The idea of a norm leads to the idea of authority. The Bible is our supreme authority. That does not mean, of course, that everything in the Bible is of *equal* authority. Our Lord indicates that in His reiterated phrase: "Ye have heard that it was said by them of old time . . . but I say unto you" (Matt. 5:21, 27, 31, 33, 38, 43). His word was of greater authority, because of greater depth, than the word of the

Old Testament. For He is, in Luther's phrase, "King and Lord of Scripture." In the last resort, He is the ultimate authority. "All authority is given unto me . . ." (Matt. 28:18).

We believe in the supernatural as the vital element in the revelation and operation of the Christian Faith.

We believe in one God eternally existing in three Persons—Father, Son, and Holy Spirit.

These articles are concerned with the doctrine of God. The first affirms His superiority to nature; the second, His triunity.

This emphasis on the supernatural was directed against the pervasive naturalism of the age, both atheistic and theistic. Atheistic naturalism, whether of the materialistic, biological, or sociological type, in affirming the reality of nature, denies the reality of God. Theistic naturalism, while affirming the reality both of nature and of God, *identifies* the two, so that there is basically but one reality which we can call nature or God as we please—the *deus sive natura* of Spinoza. Theistic naturalism is thus essentially pantheistic. And it remains so even when it forsakes the static Spinozistic type and assumes the dynamic Schellingian type which sees the whole of nature, including man, as one great evolutionary, transforming, possibly a dialectical process. God is enclosed within the closed universe of nature. He is no longer distinguishable from nature, no longer the Lord, no longer the Creator, no longer the Ruler of nature.

Over against atheistic naturalism which would deny the reality of God and over against theistic naturalism which would reduce God to the immanent processes of nature, our Statement affirms the reality of a God who is distinguishable from nature, who transcends nature, who is above nature (*supra*natural), and who therefore can be the Creator and

Lord of nature as He unquestionably is in the Bible and in classical Christian theology.

> In the beginning God created the heaven and the earth. And God said, Let there be . . . and there was. . . . (Gen. 1:1-3).
>
> Hast thou not known? hast thou not heard, that the everlasting God, the Lord, the Creator of the ends of the earth, fainteth not, neither is weary? . . . He giveth power to the faint; and to them that have no might he increaseth strength (Isa. 40:28-29).
>
> We believe in one God the Father All-Sovereign, maker of all things visible and invisible (Nicene Creed).
>
> O thou supreme, most excellent, most mighty, most omnipotent, most merciful and most just; most secret and most present; most beautiful and most strong; constant and incomprehensible; immutable, yet changing all things . . . upholding, filling, and protecting; creating, nourishing and perfecting all things . . . (Augustine, Confessions, I.iv).

This glorious, majestic, sovereign God is not unrelated to nature. He is no cold, remote, disinterested, deistic God. He is God the Creator and Redeemer, "upholding, filling and protecting; creating, nourishing and perfecting all things." He is the God who created nature; the earth with its core and its crust, its sand and its sea, its plants and its animals and man; the sun and moon and planets, the whole stellar universe with its galaxies and nebulae. He is the God who rules the universe. He is the God who created man in His own image, who provides for our needs as Father, who condemns our sins as Judge, who conquers our sins as Redeemer. Not a God who is unrelated deistically to nature and to man. Not a God who is imprisoned pantheistically in nature and in man. But a God who is above us yet near to us, a God who rules us and yet loves us, a God who condemns us and yet redeems us.

> Lord of all being, throned afar,
> Thy glory flames from sun and star;
> Center and soul of every sphere,
> Yet to each loving heart how near!
> (Oliver Wendell Holmes)

The second thing concerning God emphasized by our Statement is His triunity. God is one, yet God is three. Or rather, God is one in eternal threefoldness. Here is a mystery we cannot comprehend, yet a truth we must ever affirm. For God is one. "Hear, O Israel: The Lord our God is one Lord" (Deut. 6:4). *Deus si non unus est, non est* (Tertullian). We must never permit any trace of tritheism in our theology. Yet the Father is God, the Son is God, and the Holy Spirit is God. Hence, the one God has the threefoldness of Father, Son, and Holy Spirit. One of the loftiest expressions of this supreme mystery is to be found in that great ancient Christian poem which forms the first part of the so-called Athanasian Creed.

> We worship one God in Trinity and the Trinity in unity; not confusing the persons nor separating the substance. . . . The Father is God, the Son is God, and the Holy Spirit is God, yet there are not three Gods, but one God.

It will be noticed that this statement uses the terms "substance" and "person." These terms became standard, but have always been considered somewhat inadequate. In his work on the Trinity, Augustine frankly admits this. He writes: "When the question is asked, 'What three?' human language labors altogether under great poverty of speech. The answer 'three persons' is given not in order that it might be adequately expressed, but in order that we might not be reduced to complete silence" (*On the Trinity,* 4. 9. 10).

In the eleventh century Anselm again complains of the

poverty of human language to express the mystery, and speaks of "three, I know not what."

If the word "person" caused difficulties in the patristic and medieval periods, it causes still greater difficulties today. For it has considerably changed its meaning. It meant originally the mask or role assumed by an actor or legal representative. It denoted not a "person" in the modern sense, but the several roles which a person plays; in the case of God, the roles of Father, Son, and Holy Spirit. Today it denotes not the various roles a single person plays, but the single person who plays the various roles. It thus becomes more natural for us today to speak of the personality of the whole Godhead, rather than of the "substance" of the Godhead and the "persons" of Father, Son and Holy Spirit. Claude Welch contends that "Christianity . . . cannot be said to have been committed to a doctrine of personalities *in* God, but rather to a doctrine of the personality *of* God" (*The Trinity in Contemporary Theology,* p. 270).

It is thus understandable that there are today two schools in trinitarian terminology. The one school, represented by Althaus, Brunner, Barth, Welch, etc., prefers to speak of the personality *of God* and seeks a word other than "person" to denote Father, Son, and Holy Spirit in their distinctness. Barth has suggested the word *Seinsweisen* (ways of being). God, according to Barth, is one personal being in three ways of being, Father, Son, and Holy Spirit. The other school, represented by Webb, Champion, Hodgson, Thornton, etc., prefers to retain the traditional terminology of one substance in three persons. Eastern's Statement belongs to the second school. It speaks of "one God eternally existing in three Persons."

The difference between the two schools, however, is largely one of terminology. They basically hold the same doctrine. For both agree that the Father is God, the Son is God, and the Holy Spirit is God, yet there are not three Gods but one God. Both worship one God in Trinity and the Trinity in unity.

We believe that man was created in the image of God, and that he sinned and thereby incurred spiritual death.

Here we have, in brief, a doctrine of man. It has two main parts. First, the creation of man—"we believe that man was created in the image of God." And second, the fall of man: "we believe that he sinned and thereby incurred spiritual death."

The Creation of Man. This is, of course, but a part of the total doctrine of creation. But it is a highly significant part, for it relates to ourselves. The Statement makes a dual affirmation: first, that we were created by God, and second, that we were created in the image of God. This means that we are created *by* God *for* God—for His glory, for His service.

The Fall of Man. Similarly the statement makes a dual affirmation about our fall: First, that we are sinners, and second, that God exacts the penalty of sin, which is death.

Sin means that in practice we deny that we are created *by* God *for* God. We rebel against His lordship. We want to be our own lords. We seek our own glory rather than His. We seek dominion rather than service. We are proud rather than humble. We no longer trust God to mould our lives, but insist on moulding them ourselves. We seek freedom *from* God rather than freedom *for* God.

We thus cut ourselves off from the Fountain of Life and move toward death—not simply the death of the body, but death as the New Testament conceives it; i.e., as life under the wrath and condemnation and curse of God, both in this life and in the life to come.

Now in the late nineteenth and early twentieth century,

sin was often treated lightly and God's pardon taken for granted. The love of God was so magnified that His holiness was lost. Ideas like the wrath of God, His curse and condemnation, were regarded as barbaric relics which should be removed from Christianity. It was necessary to insist afresh on the gravity of sin, and the reality of God's condemnation, wrath, and punishment. Today, of course, the whole spiritual climate has changed; among the leading thinkers, at least, the gravity of sin and the severity as well as the goodness of God are again recognized.

We believe that Jesus Christ was begotten of the Holy Spirit and born of the virgin Mary, and that He is true God and true man, and is the only and sufficient Mediator between God and man.

We believe in the vicarious death of the Lord Jesus Christ for our sins, in the resurrection of His body, His ascension into Heaven, and His personal and visible return to the earth; and that salvation is received only through personal faith in Him.

Here is the Christological statement, the very heart of all Christian theology.

Very remarkably, the incarnation is not mentioned. It is, however, presupposed in the statement that Christ is true God and true man. Regarding the *manner* in which the Son of God became man, the Statement follows the New Testament and the almost universal tradition of the church in asserting that he came into this world, not by normal human generation, but by virgin birth of Mary through the operation of the Holy Spirit. In much modern theology the virgin birth has been and still is denied, but no good grounds are adduced for this denial.

The Statement upholds the doctrine of the New Testament and classical Christian theology that Christ is true God and true man, neither sacrificing His deity to His humanity nor His humanity to His deity. When the Statement was written, much liberal theology was in danger of losing the deity of Christ. This danger has receded, at least for the moment. Most recent books on Christology affirm Christ's true deity and true humanity.

Having affirmed that Christ is both God and man, the statement rightly calls Him the "only and sufficient Mediator between God and man." A mediator is one who stands between two who are alienated and draws them together. Christ, as both God and man, or rather as the Godman, stood between God and man who were alienated by sin, and drew them together. "God was in Christ, reconciling the world unto himself, not imputing their trespasses unto them; and hath committed unto us the word of reconciliation" (2 Cor. 5:19).

How did God in Christ reconcile the world unto Himself? Paul says it was by the death of Christ. "If, when we were enemies, we were reconciled to God by the death of his Son, much more, being reconciled, we shall be saved by his life" (Rom. 5:10). And this death of our Lord was one in which He took our place, the place of sinners, under the judgment and condemnation of God, that we might stand in His place accepted by God. "God sending his own Son in the likeness of sinful flesh, and for sin, condemned sin in the flesh" (Rom. 8:3). "He hath made him to be sin for us, who knew no sin: that we might be made the righteousness of God in him" (2 Cor. 5:21). There could be no plainer statement of that marvelous exchange in which Christ through His sufferings and death took the place of sinners in order that sinners might take His place, particularly when one remembers that the word Paul uses for "reconciliation" also means "exchange." Jesus himself had expressed the same thought when he said:

"The Son of man came . . . to give his life a ransom for many" (Mark 10:45).

All this means that Christ suffered for our sins, on our behalf and in our stead. And this is precisely what the Statement says: "We believe in the vicarious death of the Lord Jesus Christ for our sins."

Having affirmed the true incarnation and vicarious death of our Lord, the Statement goes on, like the Bible and the classical creeds of the church, to affirm His victorious resurrection, ascension, and return.

The resurrection is His victory over death. It is a victory in which His deity is demonstrated (Rom. 1:4) and our resurrection assured (1 Cor. 15:20 ff.). It is a victory which makes possible His ascension to the right hand of God (Heb. 1:3; Acts 7:56), there to intercede for sinners (Heb. 7:25) as priest and to rule over their lives as king as He lives within them (Gal. 2:20). For the ascension, though it means that Christ is no longer *visibly* present among us (Acts 1:9), does not mean that He is no longer present. Indeed, it was just before His ascension that He promised His continuing presence: "Lo, I am with you alway, even unto the end of the world" (Matt. 28:20). And it is just after His ascension that He was present with them as they preached the gospel. "So then after the Lord had spoken unto them, *He was received up into heaven, and sat on the right hand of God.* And they went forth, and preached every where, *the Lord working with them,* and confirming the word with signs following" (Mark 16:19-20). That is why after His ascension they were not dejected as after His death, but filled with joy and gladness (Acts 2:46).

Yet His presence will become all the greater and fuller when He returns visibly with great power and glory (Mark 13:26). It is this "personal and visible future return" of the

Lord, as the Statement calls it, which, combined with the doctrine of resurrection, forms the center of the Christian hope. The New Testament actually does not speak of the "return" of our Lord, since it is convinced that He has never left us. But it does speak of His coming or His visible presence (Mark 13:26; Matt. 25:6) and of our resurrection at His coming (1 Thess. 4:15 ff.; 1 Cor. 15:20-23). The Christian hope is an adventist hope. It is not centered in social and political amelioration, although Christian love leads us to be concerned with such amelioration. Nor is it centered in the millennium, which is mentioned but once (Rev. 20:3), and that once in a book filled with symbolic or pictorial language. It is centered in the visible coming of our Lord Jesus for judgment and glory in the day of resurrection (Matt. 25:31 ff.; Mark 13:26 f.; 1 Cor. 15:20 ff.; 1 Thess. 4:13 ff.) and in the consummation of His glorious kingdom (1 Cor. 15:24-28). But the time of His coming is known to God alone (Mark 13:30). Hence, we can never calculate it, but can only remain in constant readiness for it (Mark 13:33; Matt. 25:1-13; 2 Pet. 3:10).

Having set forth the great objective saving deeds of God in the incarnation, death, resurrection, ascension, and visible coming of our Lord, the Statement goes on to say that "salvation is received only by personal faith in Him." This draws attention to the subjective aspect of salvation—faith.

What is faith? It is accepting the gospel. It is receiving God's free gift of salvation in Christ. It is trusting in Christ, relying on Him and Him alone for the forgiveness of sin and victory over sin. It is committing our lives wholly to Him in trust and obedience. It is no dead faith which says "Lord, Lord" and brings forth no fruits meet for repentance, but a living faith which unites us with Christ and brings forth the fruits of the Spirit as it works through love.

How do we come to have this faith which knows Christ, which trusts Christ, which obeys Christ, and which serves Christ in love? The Statement, like the New Testament (1 Cor. 12:3), replies, Through the work of the Holy Spirit.

We believe in the personality of the Holy Spirit and that His ministry is to reveal Christ to men in the regeneration and sanctification of their souls.

This statement affirms the reality and personality of the Holy Spirit. Like Christ, He is real. Like Christ, He is personal, for He is one of the ways of being of the one personal, living God. Along with the Father and the Son, He was active in the work of creation. Hence, He is the Creator Spirit. Along with the Father and the Son, He is active in the work of redemption. Hence, He is the Redeemer Spirit. He reveals Christ to us (John 14:26; 15:26). He convinces us of sin and leads us to the Savior (John 16:8 ff.; 1 Cor. 12:3). In leading us to Him who is the Light, He illumines us; in leading us to Him who is the Life, He regenerates us; in leading us to Him who is the Mediator, He reconciles us with God and with one another; in leading us to Him who is Holy, He sanctifies us so that we belong to God and bring forth the fruits of the Spirit—love, joy, peace, longsuffering, gentleness, goodness, faith, meekness, temperance (Gal. 5:22-23).

Thus our salvation is the work of the whole Trinity, Father, Son, and Holy Spirit: the work of the Father in sending the Son and the Spirit; the work of the Son in becoming man for us men and for our salvation; the work of the Spirit in leading us to the Son. It is the work of God, and yet it involves the response of faith. "For by grace are ye saved through faith; and that not of yourselves: it is the gift of God. . . . For we are his workmanship, created in Christ Jesus unto good works, which God hath before ordained that we should walk in them" (Eph. 2:8-10).

We have spoken of faith as the fruit of the Holy Spirit. It is also the fruit of preaching. "How shall they believe in him of whom they have not heard? and how shall they hear without a preacher? . . . So then faith cometh of hearing, and hearing by the word of God" (Rom. 10:14-17). The work of the Spirit and the witness of the Word go hand in hand.

When through the external witness of the Word and the internal witness of the Spirit faith has been aroused, what is the next step? According to the New Testament, it is baptism, and entrance into the church. "Then they that gladly received his [Peter's] word were baptized: and the same day there were added unto them about three thousand souls" (Acts 2:41).

The Statement therefore goes on to speak of baptism, church membership, and the church's common meal, the Lord's Supper.

We believe that baptism is immersion of a believer in water, in the name of the Father, and of the Son, and of the Holy Spirit; setting forth the essential facts in redemption—the death and resurrection of Christ; also essential facts in the experience of the believer—death to sin and resurrection to newness of life.

This is a definition not of baptism in general but of Christian baptism in particular. It is, moreover, a normative rather than descriptive definition. It defines the mode of baptism, the subject of baptism, and the significance of baptism.

The mode of baptism is declared to be immersion in water in the name of the Father, Son, and Holy Spirit. That immersion, not pouring or sprinkling, was the original mode is clear (1) from the meaning of the Greek word *baptizo,* which means to dip; (2) from the mention of going down and coming up out of the water in the New Testament accounts of baptism (Mark 1:9 f.; Acts 8:38 f.); (3) from the significance of baptism, which is that of burial and rising from the dead.

The subject of baptism is declared to be a believer; i.e., one who has faith in Jesus Christ. The New Testament maintains a close connection between faith and baptism. On the day of Pentecost those who were baptized were those who gladly received the word of the apostle (Acts 2:41). When the eunuch asked for baptism, Philip said: "If thou believest with all thine heart, thou mayest" (Acts 8:37). (This verse is missing in some of the best manuscripts.) And it was only when the prison warden and his household believed that they were baptized (Acts 16:30-33). When Paul in his letters writes of baptism, he does so in a setting of faith. In Romans 6 he introduces the thought of baptism to demonstrate that those who are justified *by faith* (Rom. 3:21–5:21) live in newness of life (Rom. 6:1 ff.). In Galatians 3:26 f. he uses faith and baptism as parallel expressions: "For ye are all the children of God *by faith* in Christ Jesus. For as many of you as have been *baptized* into Christ have put on Christ." And in Colossians 2:12 he says: "Buried with him *in baptism,* wherein also ye are risen with him *through the faith* of the operation of God. . . ." We can scarcely evade the conclusion that in the early church there was no baptism without faith—and equally no faith without baptism. For faith unites us inwardly with Christ and baptism outwardly.

In speaking of the subject of baptism, we have answered the question concerning the significance of baptism. It is, as the Statement says, a setting forth of the death and resurrection of Christ and of the believer's death to sin and resurrection to newness of life, but it is both of these together because, through faith, it is the union of the believer with his Lord in Christ's death and resurrection.

There is today a vigorous rethinking of the doctrine of

baptism. It was started by the Paedobaptists. In 1937 Emil Brunner, lecturing in Upsala, Sweden, drew attention to the importance of faith in baptism and declared that the modern practice of infant baptism can only be described as scandalous. In 1943 Karl Barth lectured on "The Teaching of the Church Concerning Baptism." Since then we have had books on baptism by Franz Leenhardt, Oscar Cullmann, and Pierre Marcel, and a study by the Church of Scotland.

This has stimulated thought among Baptists on baptism, as evidenced by the work of Johannes Schneider of Berlin University and by the group of British Baptists who produced the book *Christian Baptism.*

We believe that a New Testament church is a body of believers thus baptized, associated for worship, service, the spread of the Gospel, and the establishing of the Kingdom in all the world.

The New Testament church, as we have seen, was composed of those who entered it by that union with Christ which we may call faith-baptism. And, as far as we can see, it was composed of such *alone*. It was a fellowship of believers in Christ, a communion of saints, the people of God, the body of Christ and the bride of Christ. The Statement is thus correct in describing the New Testament church as a "body of believers thus baptized." The Statement makes no pronouncement on the question whether the church ought always to keep this New Testament characteristic. Baptists, however, have historically maintained that it should. Hence the separation of the Anabaptists in the sixteenth and of the Baptists in the seventeenth centuries from those churches (the Lutheran, the Reformed, and the Anglican) which regarded the church as the *corpus Christianum,* the mixed community of believers and non-believers.

This body of believers, forming the body of Christ, is a

body, a living organism, in which the members are united with Christ and with one another in faith, hope, and love. They are united with their Head, Christ, in worship, in faith, in hope, in love, in obedience, and in service. And they are united with one another by their common adoration, love, and faith in Christ and by their love for one another. Moreover their love, like the love of Christ, extends beyond those who are saved to those who are unsaved. Like their Lord, they go out to seek and to save them that are lost. Evangelism becomes as much a part of their life as worship and service—indeed it is their principal service. The church is thus a redeemed, worshiping, and witnessing community which itself embodies (though in preliminary and imperfect form) the Kingdom of God, which extends the Kingdom, and looks forward to the full glory of the Kingdom at the second advent of our Lord.

We believe . . . that the Lord's Supper is a commemoration of the Lord's death until He comes.

As the church worships, serves, and witnesses between the first and second advents of our Lord, she celebrates the meal of the Lord.

As He celebrated His last passover before the crucifixion, Jesus took bread, blessed it, broke it, and gave it to His disciples, saying, "Take, eat: this is my body" (Mark 14:22; cf. 1 Cor. 11:24). Then He took wine, saying, "This is my blood of the new testament [covenant], which is shed for many" (Mark 14:24; cf. 1 Cor. 11:25). According to Paul, He added that in the future they were to take bread and wine in remembrance of Him (1 Cor. 11:24 f.).

Thus was instituted the Lord's Supper, which as the Statement correctly says, is a commemoration of His death till He comes. According to the New Testament, it is commemoration, communion, and anticipation. For it looks back to the death of our Lord, it provides communion with Christ and His people (1 Cor. 10:16 f.), and it looks forward to His return (1 Cor. 11:26).

THE RELEVANCE OF THE STATEMENT

The question of relevance may be asked from either of two points of view. We may ask whether the Statement is relevant to the Bible and the historic Christian faith, or we may ask whether it is relevant to the times. The first is the question of orthodoxy; the second, of timeliness.

Of the orthodoxy of the Statement from a Protestant and Baptist viewpoint, there can be no doubt. It affirms that the Bible is the supreme and final authority.

It affirms the supremacy and eternal triunity of God.

It affirms that man is created in the image of God and fallen from the glory of God.

It affirms the true deity and true humanity of Christ, His birth of the Holy Spirit and the virgin Mary, His sole mediatorship, His vicarious death for our sins, His resurrection, ascension, and visible return.

It affirms that we are saved solely by faith in Jesus Christ.

It affirms the personal nature of the Holy Spirit and His saving activity in revealing Christ and regenerating and sanctifying us.

It defines the nature of baptism, the Lord's Supper, and the church in terms consonant with the New Testament.

What of the Statement's timeliness? There can be no doubt of its complete appositeness at the time it was composed. It was a time, as we have seen, when the authority of the Bible, the supremacy and triunity of God, the incarnation, virgin birth, vicarious death, bodily resurrection, ascension, and return of our Lord, and the saving activity of the Holy Spirit were widely doubted or denied. It was a time when the very foundations of the faith once for all delivered to the saints were being shaken. It was a time which called for the vigorous affirmation of those foundations. This was the aim of the composers of the Statement and the founders of Eastern. The Statement admirably accomplishes this aim without bitterness, without polemics, and without entanglement in side issues.

The extent to which the Statement has been vindicated by subsequent theology is amazing. The last thirty years have seen a mighty resurgence of Biblical theology, of insistence on the supremacy and triunity of God, of a full-orbed Christology involving the incarnation, vicarious suffering, glorious resurrection, exaltation, and return of our Lord, and a renewed emphasis on faith. They have seen the questions of baptism, the Lord's Supper, and the church become central theological issues. The old liberal, modernistic, and humanistic attacks have faltered and failed.

The question therefore arises whether such a statement is still relevant today. And the answer is yes. On two grounds. First, because although the old liberalism is dead as far as theologians and professors are concerned, it is far from dead among preachers trained in the liberal tradition, and in the churches which they serve. Secondly, because new forms of liberalism may arise at any time. Paul Tillich has already spoken of a resurgence of liberalism. In this resurgence the historic Christian faith might again be threatened at one point or another. A statement such as Eastern's stands like a sentinel to discern and repulse the danger.

V

THE MIND AND THE SPIRIT

by

CARL H. MORGAN

THE DECADE PRIOR to 1925 was a period that shook America to its very depths. Except for the brief and limited Spanish-American conflict this country had experienced a half-century free from the deadly pestilence of war. In splendid isolation behind two immense ocean barriers, America rested in ease and rather smug complacency. There was no great sense of urgency in the program of the churches, or in the institutions which trained their ministers. The result was a marked decrease in the number of students preparing for the ministry, and a corresponding lack of relevancy in their theological training.

Many Christians were concerned about this alarming state of affairs. Some reacted negatively and repudiated the seminaries entirely as propagators of "the leaven of the Sadducees." These critics, for the most part, looked to the Bible schools for the training of their ministry. Others sought to recapture the lost sense of concern, but at the same time conserve the best in modern scholarship. It was this latter motive which actuated the founders of The Eastern Baptist Theological Seminary.

The story of the founding of the Seminary is presented in another chapter. Our purpose here is to explain the educational philosophy which made Eastern *worth* founding. Though the founders nowhere state their philosophy in one concise formulation, they do show clearly that they were moved with regard to the new school by four major convictions. Its educational offerings were to be (1) Biblical, (2) intellectual, (3) practical, and (4) available.

THE CENTRAL POSITION OF THE BIBLE

Several statements in the first published catalogue are important for our consideration at this point. In Volume I (1925) of the annual catalogue, we read on page 11 that the Seminary would seek to be ". . . loyal to our historic Baptist ideals and interpretation of Scriptures."

There was no question in the minds of the founders that much of the curriculum of existing seminaries was taken up with the Bible, but it was also quite clear that only a small portion of this time was given to a study of the English text with a view to its use in preaching and teaching in the local congregation. This concern for the use of the English Bible in the local church is further shown by two other statements from the first catalogue, as follows:

> "In every age the all-inclusive mission of the minister of Jesus Christ is to interpret the Word of God to the people of his own time. Whatever other demands may be made upon him . . . the minister's success depends upon his ministry of the Word. . . . The curriculum is not planned with the Bible as part of it; but rather the Bible is the curriculum. In more than

one-half of the courses, counted in hours, the Bible is studied directly. The aim is to give the student the message of the Bible. This can be gained only by studying the Bible itself. . . .

"While ample provision is made for those who care to use only the English text, the fact is not overlooked that a knowledge of the original languages of the Scriptures is absolutely essential to accurate interpretation of them. The study of these languages is required of those who seek the highest degrees in theology." (Catalogue, Vol. I, p. 30.)

Out of this desire to emphasize the importance of the English Bible grew the chair of English Bible, later endowed as the James A. Maxwell Chair of English Bible. Concerning this endowment and the chair it was stated, "In this, as in the regular sessions of the seminary, the English Bible is put at the center of the curriculum." (Catalogue, Vol. II, p. 32.) Fifteen years later we read in the catalogue for 1940 this significant statement:

"During the first two semesters the student is guided through the entire Bible. He must give evidence at the end of that period that he has read the Bible through. It is the conviction of Eastern that a knowledge of Bible content is absolutely essential to the minister, and further that critical questions should be deferred until the student is in a position to evaluate them on the basis of his knowledge of the Bible and so separate facts from theories." (Volume XV, p. 20.)

Such statements as the above could be multiplied from other published statements of the school. While these are important as an indication of convictions, they would be of little significance unless they affected practice. For the implementation of this philosophy one must look at the curriculum during the past thirty-four years.

The first catalogue shows forty-two required semester hours of Bible, including the Biblical languages, which was forty-six per cent of the curricular offerings. This was an unusually high percentage and some at that time thought it was too high. The following year (1926) shows forty-one per cent, and in 1927 it was thirty-five per cent. By this time the "shakedown" period was over and a normal percentage had been arrived at. Throughout the following years the average never fell below twenty-eight per cent (1940) and averaged 34.7 per cent. At the present time (Catalogue for 1959-60) thirty hours are required, or thirty-one per cent of the total curricular hours. This lower percentage reflects a drop in language requirements rather than fewer hours in English Bible.

The present point of view is best shown by reference to the statement on orientation to the B.D. and M.R.E. curricula as found on pages 30 to 34 of the current catalogue. In both the Department of Theology and the Department of Christian Education the *first* of the "Specific Aims" is "to acquaint students with the content, backgrounds, and methods of study of both the Old and New Testaments." In addition to these required hours, many additional elective courses in Bible are offered so that the average graduate of the Seminary comes close to achieving the ideal of the founders, namely, of having nearly one-half of his preparation directly concerned with a study of the Bible itself.

THE CONCERN FOR SCHOLARSHIP

While the founders of Eastern recognized the need for placing a study of the English Bible at the center of the curriculum, they also expressed concern for the maintenance of high intellectual standards. A study of the early minutes of the board of trustees reveals that there was some division at the beginning as to the meaning of the word "seminary." One group interpreted this word in terms of a new type of Bible

be beyond the scope of this paper to analyze them individually, or in detail as a group. A few statistics, however, may show that this concern for a trained and intellectual faculty has continued to be regarded as of great importance. Seventy-three per cent of the total have held an earned doctorate and sixty-nine per cent the master's degree. In many ways the schools from which these degrees were received present a more accurate picture of the training of these men than the degrees themselves. The doctor's degrees held by Eastern faculty members during the past thirty-four years have come from the following universities and colleges: Boston, Brown, Canisius, Chicago, Columbia, The Eastern Baptist Theological Seminary, Edinburgh, Iowa, Loyola, Maryland, Nebraska, New York, Northern Baptist Theological Seminary, Pennsylvania, Southern Baptist Theological Seminary, University of Southern California, and Missouri. Additional study has been done abroad in such universities as Berlin, Leipzig, Oxford, Edinburgh, Zurich, Heidelberg, and Manchester.

Like so many other schools, Eastern in its early days was more ambitious than wise with regard to the matter of degrees which it offered. The first catalogue indicates that the school offered work leading to ten different degrees—four in theology, three in religious education, two in missions (never granted), and one in music. By way of contrast, the 1959-60 catalogue lists three degrees—two in theology, and one in Christian education. It soon became clear that the school was "spread too thin" and the lopping off process began. Degrees in missions were never granted and missions candidates were urged to enter into the B.D. or M.R.E. courses. All certificates and diplomas were dropped, some as early as 1929, and all except music by 1939. After 1939 only two certificates were awarded to music students. So the process continued until 1952 when, with the establishment of Eastern Baptist College, the present restricted offerings were introduced. It is the conviction of the school that to maintain a high standard of scholarship it is better to concentrate its efforts in a limited area than to attempt to provide curricular offerings to meet a wide variety of interests.

However skilled and earnest the faculty may be, it is quite clear that no school can operate and maintain high standards of scholarship without an adequate library. Eastern is no exception. As everyone knows, who has had school experience, a library is a difficult thing to buy. It is something which has to be built. Eastern was both unfortunate and fortunate in this respect. It was unfortunate in that it did not inherit at the very beginning a large library. It was fortunate in that its library, starting small, has never had a large amount of "dead wood." It was the practice of the board of trustees in the early years to commission President de Blois during the summer to travel in Europe and buy books for the library. As a bibliophile of unusual taste, one who had traveled widely, and one who had studied in Germany, he was able to be wisely selective. As a result, the core of the library contained, for the most part, books which met Dr. de Blois' own high standard of excellence. Since those early days the library has grown steadily, and at times rapidly, by the purchase of a number of outstanding libraries. Among those which might be mentioned are the following: the library of Dr. Julius A. Bewer, former professor of Old Testament at Union Theological Seminary (2,000 volumes); the Princeton Theological Seminary Collection (1,500 volumes); from the Philadelphia Lutheran Seminary (700 volumes); from the Bangor Theological Seminary (500 volumes); a portion of the library of Dr. James Allen Montgomery, former professor of Old Testament at Philadelphia Episcopal Seminary and of Semitics at the University of Pennsylvania; and Migne's *Patrology* (378 volumes, others on order). In addition to these large collections which have been purchased from time to time, Eastern library has been the recipient of a number of important gift collections, such as that from the American Baptist Historical Society containing 500 volumes. The most notable gift is the Russell H. MacBride Collection. This magnificent collection of 4,500 volumes represents the result of years of judicious selection by an ardent lover of books. To make these books readily accessible, Mr. MacBride completely furnished a beautiful browsing room in which these are housed.

THE EMPHASIS ON FIELD WORK

Under the heading, "Character and Purpose of the Seminary," the first catalogue states clearly the desire to provide practical training for the students:

> "Modern life and the growing needs of our churches are making great demands upon all higher education. These demands are no less urgent upon the theological seminaries than upon other institutions of higher learning. In the organization of this Seminary, and in planning the curriculum of the four Schools, the enlarged program of our churches has been kept in mind. The Seminary maintains the highest educational standards and seeks to give the best and most practical training for the pastorate and other forms of Christian service." (Catalogue, 1925, p. 30.)

American higher education, during the closing years of the 19th century, had been greatly influenced by German scholarship. As a result, there developed a profound admiration for the meticulous thoroughness of the German Ph.D.

program. American graduate schools, using this program as a model, adapted it to the American university organization and embarked on a program of studies often described ironically as seeking "to know more and more about less and less."

The American theological seminaries, originally undergraduate departments of colleges, were just beginning to emerge as graduate institutions. Under the circumstances it was inevitable that they too should be enamored of the German Ph.D. program, with the result that the seminary training in many of our older seminaries became little concerned with the program and objectives of the local congregation and the world in which it lived. In his book, *Theological Education in America,* Kelly characterizes the seminary programs of 1870 in these words: "Generally speaking, little appeared in the program of study at this early age which had to do with any phase of religious education or the social problems of the community. All had to do with the making of the minister to serve a church which, though in the world, was quite apart from it" (p. 86).

So pronounced was this difference between the seminary world and the real world that even as late as 1908 President Faunce, in the *Lyman Beecher Lectures* delivered at Yale, pointed out that "the minister is, on ordination, usually plunged into a wholly new environment and the reaction of that environment upon his character and ideals is profound and constant." (*The Educational Ideal in the Ministry,* page 59.)

The founders of Eastern, for the most part trained in seminaries of the 19th century, were anxious to escape from these limited patterns. It was not only the theological point of view with which they found fault, but also the cold aloofness with which these seminaries viewed the problems of the average church. The ideal projected for Eastern was that it should be a place where men *served as they learned.*

There appears to have been no one on the first faculty who knew much about the basic philosophy of seminary field work, or, as it was called in those days, "practical work." This is not to be wondered at. The whole idea was very new. No more than fifteen years had passed since the first publication appeared (1910) containing a classification of medical schools and there developed a general movement within medical schools to require internship. It is not surprising that the theological seminaries, with their century-old traditions, were slower to adopt the practices of the younger medical schools.

From 1925 to 1930 there is no record of organized faculty leadership of field work. The first statement, in Catalogue, volume I, page 100, merely says: "The students are thoroughly organized for doing practical Christian services while in the Seminary. This work is now divided into five definite divisions, each with a committee. These divisions are: hospital work, Baptist Home and Orphanage work, general church co-operative work, street work, and slum and prison work. Under the leadership of these committees, the students are already functioning in a vital way in the religious life of Philadelphia and vicinity."

In 1931, the catalogue lists a committee on Practical Work of which Dr. Benjamin Livingston, professor of Evangelism, was chairman. Under this committee the Evangelistic Association functioned as the means of implementation. The stated aim was: "to keep the students occupied in various practical fields of service."

As the realization of the importance of the field work program grew, the question of academic credit for it was considered, and in 1934 a definite step in that direction was taken. By this time, all students were required to have at least one hour of practical work every week under the direction of the chairman of the Practical Work Committee. The practice of requiring monthly reports of such work was instituted at this time, a practice which is still followed. This work, when satisfactorily completed and graded, earned one hour credit for each semester.

It is worth noting that the statement in Volume X which speaks of this new step, also links placement in remunerative employment under the general heading of Practical Work. This was a rather general practice in most seminaries at that time. Three vital problems faced the director of Practical Work: (1) service to the churches, (2) the experiential needs of the student, and (3) the financial needs of the student. The pressure of necessity often put the financial needs first.

Volume XIV of the catalogue for the years 1938-39 lists for the first time a director of Field Work. The full title given to Dr. Benjamin T. Livingston was professor of Evangelism and director of Field Work. For a number of years there is no change, although the word "supervised" keeps cropping up in connection with field work statements. In 1941-42, under the subhead "Experience," one of the immediate objectives of the Seminary is stated as: ". . . to help students to develop skill in practical Christian service through a program of supervised field work." During the war years the Seminary operated on an eleven-month accelerated program. Since major emphasis had to be placed on classroom work, the program of field work suffered, but it was not discontinued. At the conclusion of the accelerated program, the faculty thought the time was ripe for a complete overhauling of the curriculum. No major changes, however, were made in field work. The item of major importance at this time was the holding of the first Conference on

Field Work in Theological Education. Following the publication of my dissertation on *The Status of Field Work in the Theological Seminaries of the United States* (1942), Professor Arthur Swift of Union Seminary approached me with the suggestion of a conference of directors of Field Work, and under the vigorous leadership of Dr. Swift and Dr. Albert G. Williams of Eastern, the first Conference on Field Work was held at Eastern in January of 1946. The stated purpose of this conference was to study "basic and essential principles and issues in current field work practice." Twenty-two seminaries were represented by their field work directors and in some cases by more than one person, and five denominational boards were also represented. To show the interest aroused, it may be helpful to list the schools represented at that first conference: Andover Newton, Biblical, Boston University, Colgate Rochester, Crozer, Drew, Eastern, Episcopal (Philadelphia), Evangelical (Lancaster), General, Harvard, Hartford, Lincoln, Lutheran (Philadelphia), New Brunswick, Pittsburgh-Xenia, Princeton, Temple, Union (New York), Union (Virginia), Western (Pennsylvania), and Yale. A second conference was held at Eastern in March of 1947 with the same number of schools (22) represented, but not in every case the same schools. New schools represented in the second conference were Augustana, Chicago, Columbia Bible College, Gettysburg, Johnson C. Smith, McCormick, Moravian, Oberlin, Seabury Western, and Warren Williamson College.

Out of this conference came a published report of proceedings, including seven papers, one written by Dr. Albert G. Williams bearing the title, "Selection, Placement, and Orientation of the Student," and one by myself bearing the title, "Certain Basic Principles of Field Work." These conferences greatly clarified the aims and methods of seminary field work and led to much revision in this area. The present picture at Eastern is this: The Seminary conceives of itself as a *graduate professional school* concerned with both sound theory and good practice. Sound theory is in general the objective of both the classroom instruction and the supervised field work, but it is recognized that these two are closely related and there is a constant attempt to integrate classroom instruction with practical experience. The following points will serve to summarize the field work program as it is at present carried on at Eastern: (1) Eastern attempts to give every student ample supervised, graded, practical experience in the work of the church. (2) Eastern's program recognizes the need of the churches. This is provided for in the Christian Service Program. Here the major emphasis is *service,* not learning, and the major control procedure is required reports. (3) Practical experience is sought under the program of supervised field work which is now integrated with two courses in Evangelism. It involves such activity as the Seminary choir, the student Evangelistic Association which holds weekly street meetings, hospital visitation which is integrated with a course in hospital ministry at the Philadelphia General Hospital and also at Lankenau Hospital, prison groups and a Youth Study Center group. (4) This program also includes practice preaching under supervision in local churches and supervisory visits by professors to the services of student pastors.

In addition to this strong emphasis on supervised field work for the students, it should be added that Eastern has always encouraged its faculty to participate actively in the work of the local churches. This point of view is based upon a definite philosophy which assumes that it is of major importance for the classroom teacher to have constant and close contact with the work of the local church. While no full-time faculty member is allowed to hold any full-time pastorate, the Seminary nevertheless constantly encourages its faculty members to accept preaching opportunities, lectureships, Bible Conferences, evangelistic meetings, and other work of the church so long as these do not interfere with the teacher's regular program of Seminary work. It is the practice of the best professional schools, both in medicine and law, to include on their faculty persons who are actively engaged in their professions. Likewise, it is the conviction of Eastern that those who are most involved in the training of ministers for the local churches must themselves become active participants in this complex and varied program. The ideal which is constantly kept before both teachers and students is that those who graduate from Eastern shall go forth with knowledge and conviction and also with adequate skill in making available their knowledge and conviction in the lives of needy men and women.

THE DESIRE TO MAKE EDUCATION AVAILABLE

Someone has wisely observed that a college needs three things: buildings, books, and brains. It can get along without buildings and, if necessary, even without books, but it must have brains or it cannot be a college. No one would have accused the theological seminaries of this country of lack of buildings, books, or trained teachers, but many of them by the second decade of this century lacked students. There were several seminaries which had more teachers than pupils. At the same time the Bible schools were growing both in number and in size. While much of the reaction against the standard seminaries came as a result of the theological gap between the churches and the schools which trained their ministers, it must not be overlooked that there were many who went to "short-cut schools" because they felt they could not meet the requirements of the seminaries. To use a commercial term, it may be said that many of the seminaries of 1920 had "priced themselves out of the market." The "price" was not high tuition fees, but higher entrance requirements and a longer training period, and to some extent disapproval of the typical American custom of "working one's way through college."

Furthermore, most of the Baptist pastors at that time were not themselves graduates of a seven-year college and seminary course. Consequently they did not encourage their young people to take what they themselves had never had.

One should not construe what has been said as a brief for "short-cut" training, but rather as an attempt to place the subsequent development of Eastern in a contemporary frame. In this connection it is interesting to note that of the members of the first entering class at Eastern, twenty-six had had Bible school training in seven different Bible schools. These same twenty-six had also had one or more years' training in nine standard seminaries, as follows: Colgate, Crozer, Newton, Northern, Southern, Southwestern, Union (New York), Western (Pennsylvania), and Xenia. These men did not choose Eastern to get a "short-cut" training.

The point might be argued as to whether Bible school credit was ever equivalent to a liberal arts course in a standard college, but the fact is that in those early days Eastern did give recognition to Bible school credit and thus was able to steer many enthusiastic young people into standard seminary training.

While the faculty in some cases accepted Bible school credit in lieu of college, the records indicate that there was growing concern over this practice. Bible school transcripts usually showed educational deficiencies in such areas as English, foreign languages, philosophy, and the physical and social sciences. In order to help overcome this weakness, two teachers were employed in 1926 to give tutoring in academic subjects. These persons were Miss Helen Maxwell, M.A., Bryn Mawr, and Rev. Edward K. Worrell, M. A., Pennsylvania. Their efforts developed into what was known as the "sub-Junior course." Classes were small and much of the work was given on a tutorial plan. Since the work was given largely on a voluntary basis without credit, attendance dwindled and by 1931 a re-evaluation was in order.

Since the reasons for starting this work had not changed, the school felt it had no alternative but to continue it. It was decided, however, to enlarge the offerings and to make credit available. Accordingly, by the spring of 1932, it was decided to establish a Collegiate Department, and Carl H. Morgan, instructor in the Department of Sacred Music, was called to organize the collegiate program and administer it. While this department began to function with the opening of the fall term in 1932, a record of this opening does not appear in the catalogue for that year since the board decision was made after the catalogue had gone to press. No collegiate courses are given in this catalogue even though twenty-three persons are listed as "collegiates." In the catalogue for 1933 the number of collegiates had risen to sixty, listed as freshmen and sophomores, and twenty-three courses are listed. The areas in which these courses were given were Bible, four hours; Philosophy, eight; French, German, Spanish, four; Greek, eight; History, eight; English, twelve; Mathematics and Physical Science, eight; Psychology, four; Speech, four.

The catalogue for 1934 contains a rather lengthy statement

of purpose prepared by the director. The following are excerpts from it:

> "The call today is for educated Christian leadership. To meet this need the educational standards of seminaries are being raised year by year. It becomes, therefore, increasingly difficult for the promising young man of limited means, or with family burdens, to enter this great and noble calling. Every year hundreds of young men who recognize the value of a higher education, are entering the active ministry with but a smattering of theological training, and no college background at all, and this through no fault of their own.
>
> "Challenged by the great opportunity for service, The Eastern Baptist Theological Seminary has established the five-year Th.B. course, the first two years of which is known as the collegiate course. The curriculum of this department has been perfected after several years of experiment and considerable research devoted to the problem of what constitutes the minimum requirement for a pre-theological education.
>
> "It is not the purpose of this department to provide a 'short cut' and all who can avail themselves of a complete four-year A.B. course are urged to do so. For those who cannot take the four-year course the Collegiate Department will provide more than the equivalent of the work done in the freshman and sophomore years of a standard college." (Catalogue, Vol. IX, p. 88.)

With the coming of President Palmer in 1936 considerable impetus was given to the growth of the Collegiate Department. Remembering the heavy financial responsibilities of his earlier years and his own struggles to complete his theological training, Dr. Palmer was deeply sympathetic with the purposes of this department. From the first year of his presidency he sought to expand its scope and enrich its offerings. This interest is reflected in a statement in the catalogue for 1937-38:

"More than five years ago when The Eastern Baptist Theological Seminary made its first departure from traditional methods of theological education by establishing the 'five-year course,' its purpose was stated as follows: '. . . to give the potential leaders of the Christian church a complete and entirely Christ-centered education.' Our conviction of the fundamental validity of this plan of education has grown with the passing years. The course has proved a success. It has attracted scores of promising men and women from High Schools to enter upon a period of intensive mental discipline and at the same time into a fellowship thoroughly Christian and passionately evangelistic.

"While the purpose of the unified Collegiate-Seminary course remains the same, its plan has been radically altered and greatly amplified. Instead of five years (for a Th. B.), the course is now six years in length (leading to A.B.-Th.B.). Instead of four days a week, it will now be five. Instead of one general course required of all, there are now four courses. The first two years are essentially the same for all courses, but in the third year the beginning of specialization appears. The four courses offered are as follows: the pre-theological course, the pre-education course, the pre-missions course, the pre-music course. At the end of the second year all students will be required to pass a series of comprehensive examinations before they will be advanced to the third year." (Catalogue, Vol. XII, p. 58.)

In 1938 the Department of Public Instruction of the State of Pennsylvania conferred upon the Seminary the right to grant the bachelor of arts degree in conjunction with the bachelor of theology for the completion of a unified six-year program consisting of four years of college work and two years of seminary work. Sixty-one students were enrolled.

In 1942 a seventh year "Honors Course" for A.B.-Th.B. graduates was set up which led to the B.D. degree. If a war had not intervened, it is quite probable that the seminary program leading to the B.D. would have become standard procedure at this time. As it was, no such change could be made because of the war-time accelerated schedule.

Though the war ended in 1945 the accelerated program could not be completed until 1947. In that year a rather thorough revision of the Collegiate Department was made and the name changed to the Theological College. Work in the college was organized into two divisions: (1) pre-seminary, offering either a major in theology or education, and (2) sacred music.

For some years prior to this, concern had been felt over the lack of recognition by the American Association of Theological Schools. Many conferences had been held with their representatives, though during this period the seminary never requested an official examination. The major point of difficulty was the anomalous position of the College Department. Though there were many cases on record of a college department of religion seeking and receiving accreditation from both college and professional associations, there was no case on record of a college department of a *seminary* being so recognized. The College Department was a foundling which neither accrediting association would adopt. The Middle States Association of Colleges and Secondary Schools insisted that it had no jurisdiction in the matter of accreditation of the department of a professional school, even if the nature of the work given was collegiate. The American Association of Theological Schools likewise protested the presence of a collegiate department as part of the Seminary. Ultimately the board of trustees came to the place where a momentous decision had to be made. To secure accreditation for the Seminary, the College Department either had to be given up or given the status of an independent corporation.

There were sharp differences of opinion both in and out

of the Seminary family, and strong arguments raised on both sides of the question. It was clear to the Board that a college could not be started on a shoestring. It would cost money and require the expenditure of an untold amount of time. Yet the results of the past years could not easily be abandoned. Many of the graduates and former teachers of the Collegiate Department had, by this time, taken leading positions in the Seminary and in the denomination. These almost unanimously pleaded for the board to continue a plan for Christian college education which had meant so much to them. The final decision was to continue in the field of collegiate training. With the close of the year 1951-52, the College Department ceased to exist and Eastern Baptist College came into being. This was a new school with a new charter, a new campus, a new dean and a new day. The wonderful growth of this college has more than vindicated the foresightedness of President Guffin and the board of trustees. It is now fully accredited by the Middle States Association and has an enrollment (1959-60) of 300 students.

Four great principles motivated the founders of the Seminary. It was their desire to place the Bible at the very heart of the curriculum and to give every student an opportunity to become acquainted with its content, the critical problems related to it, and an understanding of how the Bible could be most effectively used in the work of the gospel. It was their desire, at the same time, to lift the educational level of the Baptist ministry. They sought a school in which devotion and educational discipline would walk hand in hand. Furthermore, it was the concern of these founders that the work should be intimately related with practical experience in the churches as pastors, teachers, evangelists, and Christian educators. Finally, it was their concern that all the work which was given should be provided at the lowest possible cost and within the means of all who desired adequate education.

The passing of the years has not caused the administration of The Eastern Baptist Theological Seminary to change any one of these major concerns, though there does not appear to have been in any published catalogue of the school any statement which brings together concisely all of the data on these four major points of educational philosophy. Perhaps the best statement which has been given, and one with which this chapter may appropriately close, is that which is contained in the present catalogue under the general heading of "Operational Principles."

OPERATIONAL PRINCIPLES

"A carefully-formulated rationale underlies the curricula of Eastern. In order to prepare professional Christian leaders adequately the schools provide a well-integrated and broadly comprehensive program. Provision is made for the student's academic development, for his spiritual enrichment, and for him to develop social graces and poise. Both schools remain true to the doctrinal statement of the Seminary; they seek to practice most reliable methods coming from the field of education and provide for many practical leadership experiences for the student during his course of study.

Conservative But Not Static

"Christianity is rooted in certain historical events and documents. God revealed Himself in the writings of 'holy men of old' and finally in His Son, Jesus Christ. Revelation gives the necessary content of preaching and Christian education. Therefore, the Seminary maintains that education must be transmissive if it is to be Christian. Progressives charge that this view is a denial of the possibility of change and human progress. This Seminary answers that although truth is fixed and eternal, man's apprehension of it is finite and hence subject to continual improvement. That truth may be better apprehended is the reason for encouraging all types of research.

Authoritative But Not Authoritarian

"The School affirms the final authority of Christian revelation, but does not approve coercive teaching methods. Man is free to accept or reject authority. Belief cannot be compelled. Coercion cannot make genuine Christians. Even among Christians, differences cannot be settled by force. The teacher in this school takes his position positively and at the same time seeks to help students examine the merits and limitations of opposing views.

Theoretical and Practical

"Both the School of Theology and the School of Christian Education regard themselves as professional schools and so insist upon the interrelatedness of theory and practice. As a professional institution the Seminary seeks to prepare students for their life's work. This 'vocational' education is not of the trade-school variety whose primary function is to pass on the 'tricks of the trade.' This School conceives of good practice as issuing from sound theory, and of sound theory as always welcoming the test of practice. Students are taught not merely what to do, but why; not merely what current practices exist, but which of these are consistent with sound theory. Furthermore, students are expected to test their theory in practice.

Denominationally Related and Academically Free

"All schools are founded and supported by societies. Most American public schools are seeking to transmit the 'core values' of the supporting society, and yet are left free to give intelligent criticism of the existing order. The Seminary takes a similar position in its relation to the American Baptist Convention. It seeks to teach Baptist 'core values' without sacrificing academic freedom.

"Eastern attempts to maintain a School which is conservative but not static, authoritative but not authoritarian, both theoretical and practical, and denominationally related and yet academically free."

VI

HITHERTO AND HENCEFORTH

by

GILBERT L. GUFFIN

In the preceding chapters effort has been made not so much to write a formal history of The Eastern Baptist Theological Seminary as to record important aspects of an entrancing, and in some ways phenomenal, story. A careful historian will some day analyze all the components of this story and will set down a more complete record of the origin and ministry of the Seminary. But this will require both time for research on the part of the writer and also perhaps the revealing process which will come with the unfolding of additional years in the life of the School. In the meantime, the thirty-fifth anniversary of the institution seems of sufficient significance, and certainly the growth and service of the School during these years are meaningful enough, to warrant the telling of Eastern's record in these momentous years of national and world history, even though this must be only briefly and partially done.

These momentous years! Who can deny that the past

thirty-five years have been in many ways incomparable? To be sure, the years are not many when compared with the long span of history. But in the development of science, in the rising and falling of nations, in the shrinking of the globe itself, and in numerous other ways, there has been no period like it.

In this time an unforgettable depression, a World War which cost in life and resources perhaps as much as all previous wars combined, the spectacular Berlin Airlift, the Korean conflict (in itself a war of staggering proportions), the rape of Hungary, the development of the atomic bomb, the startling conquest of a third of the world by Russian Communism, the attainment of speed surpassing sound, and the invasion of outer space have all occurred, and these are only a few of the amazing things we have seen develop.

Dazzling as the above events have been, they are no more remarkable than what has taken place in the realm of religion and especially of Christian theology. When Eastern was born in 1925, so-called modernism, transplanted from Europe, was in full bloom in this country. Excited by the "findings" of higher critics, the vogue of many in high places was to emphasize what could not be believed about the Bible rather than to declare its great verities. Evangelism was neglected and even decried. "Rethinking" of missions, by which was meant a change of objective from that of winning a lost world to Christ to that of social improvement, considered to be the equivalent of establishing the Kingdom of God on earth, was urged. Dry rot, like that hidden in the heart of a tree, set in within the churches, a dry rot which is still blighting some areas of Christian work.

It was stalwart faith and deep conviction which led a group of men thirty-five years ago to bind themselves together under God in the establishing of a new seminary that would place the Bible at the center of its curriculum, that would make evangelism and missions major concerns of the institution, and that would declare specifically what it believed instead of insinuating what it did not believe.

It is striking to note what has happened since those days. First, there was a shattering of the dream that the world was on an escalator, moving upward inevitably toward perfection. Then there began an uneasy return—not all the way, but a long way—to the Scriptures, which led to new "discoveries" of age-old truths. Theology began again to be a concern, and more recently Biblical theology is winning increasing emphasis. Evangelism, far from being obsolete, as some had supposed, has won a new place in the sun. The Billy Graham campaigns in leading cities of the world, drawing together leaders and churches in unprecedented co-operation, are phenomenal.

Eastern believed in the unique inspiration and authority of the Bible then; it believes the same now. Eastern knew then that evangelism and missions were at the center of the Christian task; it believes the same now. Eastern believed then, when great schisms were beginning to take place in church bodies, that love of the brethren and co-operation with them, while remaining loyal to the Faith, constituted the better way; it believes the same now. Indeed, as Eastern moves toward the observance of its thirty-fifth birthday, it does so with the deep satisfaction that these years have but confirmed and endorsed its original faith and convictions. Eastern does not assume it has arrived at the ultimate of all knowledge and truth. It has an inquiring attitude and is engaged in persistent search. But it is convinced that in the Bible and in Christ there are basic and essential truths which we now know and have known and which will never change. Eastern was sure of this in 1925; it is equally certain *now*.

But what has been said above must not be taken to mean that Eastern is a static, non-progressive institution. To assume that it has been reactionary in spirit, or isolationist in attitude, or uncritical in its self-examination, or purely propositional and creedalistic in its teaching, or antiquarian in its methods, would be grossly in error.

Although the school has been fully and wholeheartedly and confidently committed to the great basic verities of the Christian faith, as emphasized earlier in this volume, it has been dynamic in attitude and progressive in practice. As one evidence of this, it was the first seminary in the Northern Baptist Convention (now the American Baptist Convention), to establish a school of Christian Education. Since then all the seminaries of the American Baptist Convention have incorporated Christian Education in their programs. Eastern was one of the first seminaries in the nation to develop a field work program, the precursor of the present clinical training programs common to all progressive seminaries. As elsewhere related in this volume, Dean Morgan's *The Status of Field Work in the Protestant Theological Seminaries of the United States* (1942), became the original resource material for seminaries in developing field work, and Eastern was host to the first two national conferences of seminary representatives regarding this type of service.

In these and in many other ways Eastern has been not only progressive and dynamic, but creative and pacesetting. Nor has Eastern been unaware of changing emphases and new formulations of thought in various fields, such as in theology and in Biblical studies. Its professors have kept abreast of them, but through all the transitions of thought in these areas, however, Eastern has had a basic conviction, a solidarity of faith, and a depth of understanding which have kept her from becoming the victim of every vagary that has appeared and have restrained her from a will-o'-the-wisp chasing of every new philosophical or theological idea that has come along, whether that idea accorded with divine revelation and the experience of the Church or not. Thus, Eastern has been both conservative and progressive, both authoritative and dynamic; both positive and constructive. It has never been, as President de Blois used to declare, "polemical or invidiously controversial."

EASTERN'S PRESENT POSITION

Previous chapters have noted some of the past achievements of Eastern and have suggested something of its present strength. A further detailing of the latter may now be justified.

Measured by her academic strength, her relationship and service to the churches, the caliber of her students and alumni, the standing of her faculty, and the quality of her facilities, Eastern compares favorably with the better seminaries of the country.

A comparative analysis of the 82 accredited seminaries related to the American Association of Theological Schools shows Eastern to stand as follows:

	"Average" Seminary	*Eastern*
Enrollment	230	228
Full-time Faculty	14	14
Part-time Faculty	5	11

Of these 82 schools, in 1958-59, 33 had an enrollment larger than Eastern's; 48 a smaller enrollment.

But mere comparison of Eastern with the average of ac-

credited seminaries of the country in number of students, size of faculty, etc., only partially reveals the strength of Eastern. Of more importance, for example, is her academic position. This may be indicated by the fact that Eastern has threefold accreditation: by the American Association of Theological Schools, by the Middle States Association of Colleges, and by the American Association of Schools of Religious Education. So far as is known, no other Baptist seminary is accredited by all three of these agencies.

The academic recognition of Eastern by sister seminaries is attested by the large number of schools which have called faculty members from Eastern or have engaged Eastern's alumni for service. A check reveals that eight American Baptist, three Southern Baptist, and at least five other seminaries presently are using or have used Eastern faculty members or graduates for faculty or administrative positions. In a half dozen or more of these cases, the president has been or is now an Eastern alumnus. Moreover, Eastern alumni are now serving or have served on the faculty or staffs of eighteen or more colleges and universities. The presidents of such well-known schools as Oklahoma Baptist University, Alderson-Broaddus College, Goshen College and Seminary, and Bethel College and Seminary are graduates of Eastern.

The ratio of Eastern's faculty to students is about 1 to 11. With 14 full-time professors and 11 part-time, Eastern has a strong teaching force. The 14 full-time faculty members hold 19 doctors degrees and have had an impressive total of about 216 years (average of 15 years each) of teaching experience, besides many years of service in pastorates or on mission fields. As in the past, Eastern's faculty continues to write for important journals, to publish books, and to lecture widely.

Eastern's alumni, who now number 1,451 full graduates (not including those who have studied at Eastern but did

not earn degrees), serve nearly 1,000 churches in our own and other denominations as pastors, Christian education directors, or music directors. The others are working on mission fields, as denominational officials, chaplains, teachers, school administrators, and the like. The largest percentage of these are in the American Baptist Convention. A survey made by the Commission on the Ministry of the American Baptist Convention in 1957, and revised in 1958, reveals that Eastern had the second largest number of alumni of any seminary serving as pastors in the Convention, despite the fact that all but one of the other seminaries of the Convention are older than Eastern. The one seminary having a larger number of alumni in the pastorates of American Baptist Convention churches is more than 100 years older than Eastern.

Among leading churches which have been served at different times by Eastern alumni are Tremont Temple, Boston; Baptist Temple, Philadelphia; Temple Baptist, Los Angeles; First Baptist, Seattle; First Baptist, Portland; First Baptist, Lincoln; First Baptist, Topeka; First Baptist, Waterloo; First Baptist, Detroit; First Baptist, St. Paul; First Baptist, Plainview; First Baptist, San Diego; First Baptist, Pomona; National Memorial Baptist, Washington; and First Baptist, Calgary, Canada; as well as a number of outstanding churches in other denominations.

Eastern's alumni are reported presently to outnumber those of any other seminary in our Baptist work in Pennsylvania and in New Jersey, and are numerous in such other states as New York, Massachusetts, Maine, Ohio, Illinois, Maryland, the District of Columbia, and California. Indeed, they serve in 49 of the 50 states of the Union, including Alaska and Hawaii. They also serve in 26 foreign countries including Africa, Argentina, Belgium, Brazil, Burma, Canal

Zone, Canada, China, Costa Rica, Dutch New Guinea, El Salvador, England, Equador, France, Haiti, India, Indo-China, Iraq, Italy, Japan, Philippines, Portugal, Porto Rica, Spain, Thailand, and Venezuela.

The number of known denominational posts held by Eastern graduates since 1925 is indicated by the following totals:

a. Members of National Boards and Committees ... 63
b. National Staff members 14
c. Executive Secretaries of State Conventions 11
d. State Staff members 35
e. City Society executives and staff 17

Eastern's student body each year comes from 130 to 160 different colleges and universities in this and other countries. They are required to have good academic records for admission, and they must make good grades to remain. Total enrollment has run from 185 to 228 per year for the past several years, not including summer school, which totaled 102 the past summer (1959).

Eastern is fortunate not only in the quality of its faculty and the caliber of its alumni and students, but also in the desirability of its location. Beginning on famous Rittenhouse Square in Philadelphia, it was relocated in 1940 under the wise leadership of President Gordon Palmer on the well-known Green Hill Farms property at Overbrook, in suburban West Philadelphia at the junction of cross-country routes 1 and 30 and at the junction with the city of the famous Main Line of Philadelphia. But more important than this is the fact that Eastern is located in the city where the first organized Baptist work in this land was begun. The Philadelphia Baptist Association, the oldest in America, was established in 1707. Here much of the rest of the work of Baptists in this country had its inception. Here (at nearby Valley Forge) the new headquarters of the American Baptist Convention will be located. Eastern considers itself fortunate to be situated in this historic Baptist center, famous also for its Independence Hall and for being the seat of the early government of this country. Here historic lore, national and religious, blends with a high level of culture to make this a choice center of learning.

The present facilities of Eastern consist of six splendid buildings, whose book value is nearly two million dollars, but whose estimated insurance value is in excess of three and one-half million dollars, not counting the value of the land. These buildings, colonial in design (except for the last-named), are Gordon Palmer Hall, a residence and administration building that was formerly an exclusive residential hotel; the Austin K. de Blois Library, capable of housing around 100,000 volumes and presently containing a select library collection of over 60,000 volumes; the Curtis Lee Laws Chapel and William Howard Doane Hall of Music and Education, built in 1951 at a cost of over $400,000.00; Eastern Hall, where there are fifty-six apartments for married students and adjacent to which is a large fenced-in playground; the Lancaster Apartment Building for faculty residences; and the home of the president. The last three buildings are off campus, but are conveniently located.

A further factor in Eastern's present strength is the endowment which has been accumulated, chiefly as a result of the stewardship and Christian devotion of friends of the school and the competent management by the officers of the board of trustees and the administration. As is now well known, Eastern was the fortunate recipient at the time of its founding of a magnificent gift from an anonymous source of approximately $500,000.00, which through increase of value soon rose to $1,000,000.00 and more. The present book value of the endowment is $1,751,758.00, but the market value, which, of course, fluctuates, is much larger. This is far from enough for the needs of the school, but income on these investments is a great assistance in these days of rising costs and of expansion. In fact, returns on this endowment last year amounted to $165,000.00 toward the total expenses of the year of $350,000.00. Though no greater income can be anticipated from this source unless endowment is increased, expenses continue to rise.

Moreover, the rise in expenses cannot reasonably be overcome by increasing student fees. In fact, there seems to be a definite limit to which a seminary may go in raising fees. One reason is that seminary students seldom are able to depend on parents for their continued support as do college students. Frequently all their resources have been exhausted by the time they reach a seminary. Then too these students now more often than not are already married and in many cases have one to three children to support. What resources they can raise are thus required for family use. To make the condition even more difficult, these students cannot afford to borrow money for their seminary training, even if they could find a source from which to borrow. The simple reason is that unlike their medical, engineering, or other counterparts, they will receive usually such small salaries from the churches that it would be almost impossible for them to repay a loan. Few churches, furthermore, would be likely to consider calling a pastor who had a considerable debt hanging over him when he leaves school. Hence Eastern cannot expect to take care of the ever-increasing cost of its operations without either greatly enlarged endowment or greatly increased income from gifts, or both. Therefore, although the amount of the present endowment is most gratifying, the seminary hopes it will be significantly enlarged in the years ahead.

A recapitulation of the financial assets of the Seminary reveals the following significant totals as of the end of the past fiscal year (June, 1959):

	Book Value	*Estimated Real Value*
Plant	$1,780,498.59	$3,500,000.00 (not
Library holdings	145,671.61	including land value)
	$1,926,170.20	
Endowment	$1,783,153.66	
TOTAL	$3,709,323.86	

If to the above are added the present assets of Eastern Baptist College, which was founded by the Seminary, an even more impressive figure will be noted.

The College now has plant assets of about $1,500,000.00 (book value) and endowment of $688,000.00 (book value). These combined with the above totals would make a grand total—using book values of the Seminary endowment and plant—of approximately $5,897,000.00. Of course, current market values would be considerably higher than this. It seems nothing short of miraculous that from the original gift of $26.00, obtained by Dr. John A. Hainer from the Blockley Baptist Church as the initial contribution for the starting of the Seminary, the assets of the Seminary and its daughter school, Eastern Baptist College, could in the short span of thirty-five years have risen to such a sizable figure as the above total. Much has been added by many people to that original offering from the Blockley Church. Without taking any credit from those who, out of love and a sense of Christian stewardship, have given in both large and small amounts, it seems proper to acknowledge that the phenomenal record of Eastern's growth is the Lord's doing and it is marvelous in our sight.

A breakdown of the budgets of the current year (1959-60) and a comparison of the totals for the year of 1948-49 with the totals for the present year reveal considerable increases, as will be seen below. (The budget of the year of 1949-50 is also given below, but it does not afford a good comparison because it was for a period of thirteen months, which was to accommodate a change in the beginning of the fiscal year from April 30 to May 31.)

	1959-60	*Budget Totals*
Income		
Educational and General		
Endowment		$166,056.00
Student fees		37,825.00
Gifts		50,700.00
Other sources		24,260.00
Auxiliary Enterprises		74,000.00
	Total	$352,841.00
Expenditures		
Educational and General		
General Administration		$ 77,788.00
Instruction		114,838.00
Library		27,307.00
Operation and Maintenance		81,120.00
Auxiliary Enterprises		29,142.00
Other Expenses		22,377.00
	Total	$352,572.00

	1948-49
Income	$215,109.48
Expenditures	$202,504.62

	1949-50 (13 months)
Income	$251,545.15
Expenditures	$244,116.76

It will be seen from the above that all student fees of this year represent only about 10 per cent of the total anticipated income. This was true also of other recent years. It may further be noted that the "gifts" item in the present budget is a much larger figure than student fees. Moreover, if gifts should fall short of the estimate, a great difference would result in the possibility of the School's being able to meet its actual expenses of the year.

That the total budget of the School, though far greater than it was even ten years ago, is a modest one may be indicated by the fact that some other seminaries of relatively the same size have budgets larger than Eastern's by $100,000.00 or more.

A parenthetical paragraph may appropriately be inserted here to emphasize how fortunate Eastern has been from the early days when Ralph Levering, elsewhere mentioned, served as Treasurer until the present in having men unusually competent in finance to supervise this aspect of her work. Dr. Harvey Bartle succeeded Mr. Levering on the latter's death and has for fifteen years—since his retirement as head of the Pennsylvania Railroad Medical Service—administered the finances of the school. Moreover, Dr. Charles S. Walton, Jr., for the past twenty years the able and dedicated chairman of the board and a person remarkably gifted in the areas of investments and finance, has given close and constant attention to this phase of Eastern's development. To these men especially, as well as to the finance committee and the board as a whole, Eastern is mostly indebted, humanly speaking, for an enviable record in meeting its obligations as well as measuring up to the increasing demands growth and inflation have made upon the School. Never have the faculty or staff had to wait for their salary checks, nor has the school more than once or twice closed a fiscal year "in the red."

In recent years, of course, because endowment income has not increased sufficiently to take care of growing needs, the gap between income and expenditures has been filled only because there has been a constantly enlarging income from the gifts of churches, alumni, and friends. A vigorous program of public relations has been a vital factor. Something of the growing necessity of this program may be suggested by the fact that in 1944 when Dr. Bartle became Treasurer the total budget of the Seminary and the Collegiate Department, then combined with the Seminary, was only $125,-000.00. This year the operating budget of the Seminary alone is about $352,572.00, and the budget of Eastern Baptist College about $450,000.00, or a total of over $800,000.00; and this does not include capital outlay. To those who have helped so significantly in making such a record possible, and above all to the Lord Himself, all who love Eastern will be abidingly grateful.

In assessing the present position of Eastern, no record would be complete which did not note the continuing determination of Eastern to be loyal both to Christ as the rightful Head and Lord of the school, and to the Bible as the inspired and authoritative Word of God. In this determination, combined with the faith of those who have had a part in the founding and leading of the school, it is believed, lies the institution's chief basis of strength. No matter what or how much could be included in an inventory of Eastern's assets, if loyalty to Christ and to the Word could not be included, the school would feel itself to be poor indeed. And if to these basic loyalties the strength of great, unwavering faith be added, is not this the victory that "overcomes the world"?

EASTERN'S FUTURE PROSPECTS

All that has preceded in this volume has dealt with either the past that is history or with the present that is visible reality. It now seems appropriate to ask, What are the future prospects of Eastern Seminary?

To assume the role of the seer is responsible if not hazardous business.

"My gran'ther's rule was safer'n 'tis to crow:
Don't never prophesy—onless ye know." (Lowell.)

Obviously it is not possible for one to know positively what the future holds for Eastern, but as "coming events cast their shadows before" (Campbell) and as "in today already walks tomorrow" (Coleridge), it is possible on the basis of past achievements and present realities to make certain forecasts with a reasonable degree of accuracy. For example, by using the statistical method one can make a fair estimate as to probable advances in enrollment, endowment, and campus facilities. A check of the records reveals that in the year 1950-51 there were 74 B.D. students enrolled. Last year (1958-59) there were 124. (Neither number, of course, includes the M.R.E. and Th.M. students.) A similar growth in the next ten years would bring the number to approximately 200 B.D. students alone. In 1949-50, the total enrollment of the Seminary (not including the Collegiate Division and a few candidates for the doctor's degree then being given, but including Th.M. students) was 113. Last year it was 205 for the first term, and it rose to a total of 228 for the year (not including a summer school enrollment of 102). Similar development in the next few years would seem to indicate a possible enrollment of around 300 in the not far distant future. Of course, such growth depends on several uncertain factors, the chief one being the potential sources of students. Although certain recent surveys seem to indicate a tragic decline in the number of young men and women going into full-time specialized Christian service, it is hoped that this is only a temporary recession and will soon pass.

In the past ten years the Seminary has spent approximately $900,000.00 on purchasing and reconditioning or on erecting new buildings and making other campus improvements (not counting its investment in the founding of Eastern Baptist College). Fortunately the Seminary now has facilities with one or two exceptions to accommodate up to 300 students. These exceptions are the need of more apartments for married students and probably of additional housing for faculty members. The increasing numbers of students who marry before coming to the seminary call for special provisions for them. To meet this condition, Eastern like other seminaries, it appears, will have to provide additional quarters for apartments. A second faculty apartment structure may also be necessary.

Though it is not now contemplated that for some years ahead a great deal of campus development will be required, the same cannot be said for the resources of the school. A growing student body, the expansion and enrichment of curriculum that is already envisioned, and the anticipated restoration of graduate work leading to the doctor's degree, together with constantly rising costs in general, will demand greater income than is presently being obtained. Though faculty salaries have been increased as much as 55 per cent in the past ten years, they are still too low. Plans have been authorized by the Board for considerable advance. This will require additional resources. Funds are greatly needed also for the enlargement of library holdings, for scholarships, and for lectureships. Very likely an annual operating budget of a half million dollars will soon be a necessity, and in ten years the budget may reach a million dollars. Enlargement of endowment as well as increase of income through gifts from churches and friends seems imperative.

The past steady advance of Eastern in its service to the denomination and to Christian leadership in general will undoubtedly continue in the future. With its major emphasis on the preparation of men for the work of the pastorate, Eastern also puts great weight on the training of men and women for the work of missions at home and abroad and for Christian education leadership. All of this will be vigorously pursued in the future. An increasing number will also be trained for the work of teaching in Christian schools, for the chaplaincy, and for related ministries, such as denominational leadership and religious editorial service.

Indeed, continued growth seems to be indicated for Eastern, even as the need for the kind of product Eastern produces will continue to exist. Eastern has no intention of resting on its oars. The same vital, dynamic spirit that has characterized her past and marks her present will certainly distinguish her future.

No look at Eastern Seminary's future should omit the possible significance in the days ahead of the relationship of that institution to Eastern Baptist College. As elsewhere stated, Eastern Baptist College was formerly a collegiate division of the Seminary. In 1952 the Seminary had this collegiate division incorporated as a full liberal arts college and enabled it to be relocated on its own remarkably beautiful campus, eight miles away, at St. Davids. Though this growing college is a totally separate institution, it operates as a sister (or daughter) school with close natural ties to the Seminary. The latter looks upon the College as in effect an extension of its own ministry, at the undergraduate level, to youth, and hence to the denomination and to the cause of Christ at large. To establish this College was a source of some strain to the Seminary for the first few years of the latter's history, but the need for the College was so compelling as to make this strain seem an undeniable obligation.

This is an appropriate point at which to restate the financial terms under which the College was established. Particularly is this advisable when it is recalled that at the time the College was incorporated it was suspected by some that the Seminary had been weakened by this step. It was supposed by those who made this assertion that a very large part of the assets of the Seminary was required for setting up the College. The truth is that although the enrollment of the Collegiate Division of the Seminary at the time of the separation move was nearly equal to that of the Seminary, and although this Division dated back to 1932 officially and even earlier than that in informal character, and although this Division on theses counts would have been entitled to a greater share of the assets of the Seminary, it was decided by the board and administration that only one-fifth of these assets (at the market value of that date) should be given to the College for its endowment. This was only a little more than the minimum required by the State of Pennsylvania for the setting up and incorporating of a college in the State. This decision was dictated by the conviction that the Seminary as the mother institution should not be weakened by the College, and by the further conviction that the College would be able in a few years to meet its own financial needs through the larger tuition it could warrantably charge and through resources it would very likely obtain in its own right, and that it would be able to do this more easily perhaps than would be possible for the Seminary. Subsequent years have proved the wisdom of this conclusion. The College now has, and has had from its incorporation, a totally separate financial structure and now bears its total financial responsibility.

Of course, the Seminary assisted the College in the purchase of its present magnificent site. But the total cost of the purchase of the three estates which made up the original campus of the College and the reconditioning and furnishing of the buildings there for the opening of the College in its new setting in 1951 cost less than the new chapel built at the Seminary at about the same time.

Furthermore, the separation of the collegiate program from the Seminary relieved the latter of the expense of the collegiate faculty, staff, etc., which was taken over by the College. This expense had actually been much larger than the income from the amount of endowment the Seminary gave the College. Thus despite the gift of one-fifth of its endowment to the College, and the Seminary's assistance of the College in the original purchase of its campus, the Seminary was financially better off so far as operating expenses were concerned as a result of the move. In fact, the income on the total amount given to the College for endowment and purchase of a campus was really only about half of the cost of faculty and staff salaries for the Collegiate Division. At that time the Seminary was spending $65,000.00 to $70,000.00 annually on these salaries alone, besides the other costs incidental to the operation of the Collegiate Division. At the time of the decision to separate the collegiate program from the Seminary the total income from all the funds provided the College was only about $35,000.00 per year. In one sense, therefore, it was a move of economy to allow the College to become a separate institution, even if in doing so a considerable sum of money had to be given the College. To be sure, an alternative would have been to discontinue the Collegiate Division altogether, but the need for a school such as Eastern Baptist College in this region, especially among Baptists, plus the fact that a strong faculty and an excellent academic program of tested strength, over a period of twenty years, already existed in this Collegiate Division, made such a course seem utterly unjustifiable. Moreover, the trustees after prolonged prayer and thought felt divinely led to undertake the development of the College and also felt that although it was a great step of faith, this faith would be justified. The subsequent growth of Eastern Baptist College has seemed to confirm this conviction. Since the College was established it has enjoyed more than a 300 per cent increase in its enrollment and is receiving ever-widening recognition.

It has been obvious to those who have had the facts that the founding of the College did not weaken the Seminary. Indeed, the separation of the collegiate program from the Seminary has appeared to be decidedly beneficial to both institutions. It is confidently believed that the steady and rather certain growth of the College in both academic strength and influence, as well as in the outreach of its service, will indirectly if not directly return dividends of great and increasing value to the Seminary.

The only condition the Seminary made regarding the financial assistance it gave to the College was that if the latter should ever cease to hold to the purpose for which it was founded, and especially if it should depart from the doctrinal basis on which it was established, all the assets of the College should revert to the Seminary. This decision was made because of the determination of the trustees that Eastern Baptist College should be as well guarded as possible from the tendency which has so often marked other colleges founded with high Christian commitments, namely to drift away from their original purpose.

In contemplating the future, one may be sure that above all Eastern will continue to hold faithfully to the great centralities of the Faith. Though certain theological formulations may change and deeper conceptions in certain areas will be inevitable, Eastern is sure that the great basic foundations of Christian belief will stand unshaken. It is sure also that the conviction it holds will be pertinent for the needs of the future. It is also aware of the grave responsibility which will rest upon it in the days ahead.

Admittedly, there are problems of gravest character confronting all theological seminaries in these times. Perhaps we should not speak of "problems" but "exacting opportunities." It is significant that the Bible nowhere uses the word "problem"; it does speak of "trials," "hardness," "burdens," and "afflictions." Whether the issues seminaries confront are called "problems" or "exacting opportunities," they are nonetheless challenges of great magnitude. All theological seminaries, like all believers, are confronted with the present-day challenge to faith itself, the challenge to moral standards, the challenge to integrity, the challenge to discipline and authority, and the challenge to peace and international understanding. The seminaries which hold basically to the historic New Testament view are confronted with all the above challenges plus a number of others, such as the challenge to a belief in the supernatural, to adherence to the Trinitarian conception of the Godhead, and to the fellowship of Christians in a day of multiple divisions which fragmentize the visible church and cause "blemishes"—to use Paul's metaphor in Ephesians—on the Body or Bride of Christ. Moreover, certain seminaries which believe that the New Testament requires them to be deeply concerned for the salvation of the lost in all the world are also confronted with a challenge to their convictions regarding evangelism and the work of missions. Because of Eastern's basic theological position it is confronted with all of the above challenges. As a Baptist seminary (though, of course, it readily admits students of all evangelical denominations), it is also confronted with the present colossal challenge to freedom, to soul liberty, to the separation of church and state, and to the idea of a regenerate church membership. Though our forefathers struggled valiantly in order that certain rights, for example, freedom of worship and freedom of speech, might be guaranteed to all men, not just to themselves, we have seen occasions recently when in some places men, far from having freedom of speech, did not have freedom even to be silent! Many have had to shout "me too" or be condemned. Eastern cannot be true to its commitments without concern that such challenges exist and without throwing all of its strength into an effort to overcome them.

In other words, Eastern shares most if not all of the burdens which all seminaries bear in these days. It shares additional ones which are peculiar to seminaries of theologically conservative convictions. It carries still others because of its typically Baptist position. All of this is to say that Eastern is aware—at times almost agonizingly aware—of its responsibilities in the future, even as it has been aware of its responsibilities in the past. It simply must face up to all the above challenges. The commitment it has made to the full and rightful Lordship of Christ allows for nothing less.

But other responsibilities also concern Eastern as it looks to the future. The health and prosperity of the Philadelphia Baptist Association is one of these. In this great historic and rapidly growing metropolitan area over 4,000,000 people reside, more than one million of whom are reported to belong to no church or synagogue. Perhaps fewer than half of them could really be called Christians in any strict sense. It is a vast melting pot of racial and national backgrounds. Baptists, simply because they are second only to Roman Catholics in numerical strength in this area (including, of course, both white and Negro Baptists), have a major responsibility. Eastern cannot and does not wish to escape its involvement. Nor can Eastern escape the grim fact that the Baptists of Philadelphia, to whom this Seminary is so closely related, are not making such forward strides in evangelism and church building as would indicate their being fully awake to their responsibility.

While Eastern Seminary is not under the control of the American Baptist Convention, it is directly related voluntarily and is a recognized seminary of the denomination. It, therefore, cannot forget the saddening fact that the convention has seemed for some time, so far as total membership is concerned, to be standing still or even declining in strength. In a day of burgeoning population and indescribable opportunity, Eastern feels a great burden over this condition. If it could be proved that the cause of Christ and especially the evangelizing of this nation would be strengthened by the decline of American Baptists, then Eastern could be reconciled to the decline. But the truth must be the opposite of this. The fact that most other Baptist bodies in this country are growing and that Baptists as a whole in the United States have increased from around 4,181,000 in 1900 to over 19,000,000 as of the present can be no consolation to her as long as American Baptists are winning to Christ fewer than they are losing by death and withdrawal.

Eastern was established to be a constructive and evangelizing force within the denomination. "In common with all Baptist leaders who love our denomination," said the founders of Eastern in a policy statement of the school, "we believe that our Baptist work should be done through the denomination itself and its constituted agencies." The statement continues: "We believe that the great body of Baptists is evangelical in faith and loyal to the denomination, and it is the purpose of the Seminary to promote evangelical faith and denominational loyalty."

Committed to the above policy, as the Seminary has continued to be, it cannot avoid a sense of deepest concern for the health and the evangelistic fervor of the Baptists with whom it is immediately associated. Eastern is convinced that only as any Christian body, whether it be a local congregation or a whole denomination, is possessed of a warm evangelical faith, that only as it is motivated by a clear New Testament conception of the lostness of men and of the saving power of Christ and of Him alone, will it pursue with ardor the work of evangelism. Eastern is also convinced that only as a denomination, or as Christians as a whole, pursue with zeal the work of evangelism, with all that is included in that task, is there a chance of extending their boundaries into the mighty, widening seas of unbelief in this day or in the future. The non-Christian part of the world is now outgrowing all Protestant and Evangelical bodies of Christians combined at a rate of fifteen to one. Christians and especially Baptists dare not get bogged down in mere organization when they should be a triumphant movement.

EASTERN'S PREMISES FOR PROGRESS

The premises upon which Eastern bases its hope of progress in the future are:

a. Faith in God.
b. Fealty to the Lord Jesus Christ.
c. Faithful adherence to Biblical truth.
d. Fellowship of believers: an attitude of co-operation within the denomination, as well as a determination to find ways of co-operation with all Christians.
e. Fulfillment unceasingly of its original mission: "The whole gospel for the whole world."

In the early days of the school, President de Blois declared the purpose of the Seminary to be, "To prepare ministers of symmetrical competency, intellectually qualified and spiritually devoted, and inflamed by the fires of a pure and thoroughly evangelistic passion."

Referring to the conviction of the founders of the school, Dr. de Blois stated, "It was believed . . . that the time had come for the establishment of a new, splendid intellectual propaedeutic that should develop a noble loyalty to the basic spiritual principles of the gospel, and that should secure a dominating and permeating evangelistic purpose as the supreme motif in the training of men for the Christian ministry."

This same conviction still pervades and motivates, and will continue to pervade and motivate, the trustees, the faculty, and the administration. Indeed, it may be said now as Dr. de Blois so aptly put it years ago:

> "The purpose of Eastern Seminary is clear as sunlight. It has been the inspiration of the school's astonishing power and growth. The purpose is to train and equip the future ministry of our denomination in scholarly character and fidelity to revealed truth, so that they may become stalwart leaders of our churches and effective prophets of the Most High."

Eastern is borne onward by an exalted and holy purpose. It is moved by a profound conviction that the only moral and spiritual hope for man in the space age now apparently dawning, as it has been in all ages past, is the redemption offered him through Christ. In this purpose and conviction Eastern marks this anniversary and indeed will press on beyond its thirty and fifth birthday, resolved under God to continue not merely to work within history but also to "make" history to the praise of the glory of Him whose Name is above every Name.

APPENDIX

THE BOARD OF TRUSTEES

Charter Members

1925-26	*CHARLES T. BALL	*Philadelphia, Pa.*
1925-41	*JOHN A. HAINER	*Philadelphia, Pa.*
1925-30	*HARRY WATSON BARRAS	*Haddonfield, Pa*
1925-30; 39-	THORNLEY B. WOOD	*Philadelphia, Pa.*
1925-	RALPH L. MAYBERRY	*Philadelphia, Pa.*
1925	*FRANK M. GOODCHILD	*New York, N. Y.*
1925-47	*CURTIS LEE LAWS	*New York, N. Y.*
1925-39	*JAMES A. MAXWELL	*Chester, Pa.*
1925-44	P. VANIS SLAWTER	*Trenton, N. J.*
1925-27	E. B. DWYER	*Kittanning, Pa.*
1925	*DAVID LEE JAMISON	*Albany, N. Y.*
1925-	GORDON H. BAKER	*Schenectady, N. Y.*
1925-27	†JOHN E. BRIGGS	*Washington, D. C.*
1925-26	FRANK EARLE PARHAM	*New York, N. Y.*

* Deceased.
† Emeritus.

Former Members

1955-58	Ronald K. Adams
1952	John A. Baird, Jr.
1949-58	James Barnes
1944-56	John Binns
1947-52	Edwin H. Castor
1925	John B. Champion
1939-52	Anthony H. Clarke
1930-48	Martin F. Clough
1927-46	Austen K. de Blois
1925-29	Mrs. Carl Gray
1955-59	John G. N. Henderson
1925-32	Joseph W. Hill
1925-49	Wesley H. Hoot
1931-35	Will Houghton
1925-40	Joseph Y. Irwin
1947-56	Mrs. Curtis Lee Laws
1939-40	Mrs. Eugene Levering
1925-43	Ralph I. Levering
1928-40	David R. Miller
1927	Mrs. I. H. O'Hara
1940-46	Verner I. Olson
1926-27	Charles W. Parson
1946-55	Norman W. Paullin
1927-47	Mrs. Lucy W. Peabody
1940-59	Earle V. Pierce
1935-58	Harry B. Reinhart
1927-28	F. P. Ristine
1934-44	Col. Ernest Rogers
1925-26	Lawrence N. Sirrell
1930-34	H. Theodore Sorg
1925-37	Alonzo R. Stark
1929-32	Walter A. Staub
1935-51	Walter Theodore Taylor
1939-51	Carey S. Thomas
1940-53	Henry W. Tiffany
1928-43	Charles R. Towson
1937-48	Joseph Twomey
1929-34	R. J. Wadsworth
1925-29	William H. Waite
1954-58	Ralph C. Walker
1934-45	Joseph Thomas Watts
1958-59	William F. Weber, Jr.

Present Members

1945-	Paul E. Almquist, Vice-Chairman
1939-	William Ward Ayer
1925-	Gordon H. Baker, Secretary
1959-	Omar N. Barth
1932-	Harvey Bartle, Treasurer
1956-	John W. Bradbury
1955-	Frank K. Brasington
1925-	John E. Briggs (Emeritus)
1955-	Benjamin P. Browne
1939-	C. Gordon Brownville
1957-	Charles Coleman, Jr.
1948-	Hubert A. Davidson
1955-	John C. Dettra
1944-	S. Raymond Estey
1952-	William H. Evans
1956-	Harold L. Fickett, Jr.
1952-	Alger W. Geary
1941-	Gilbert L. Guffin
1925-	William P. Haug
1959-	Walton M. Henry
1943-	Harry L. Jenkins
1959-	Clifton E. Mack
1925-	Ralph L. Mayberry
1943-	Clifford C. Meeden
1955-	Frank Middleswart
1936-	Gordon Palmer
1954-	Elmer F. Ruark
1959-	H. Richard Stevens
1953-	Calvin I. Swayne
1959-	Joseph A. Vettel
1959-	Peter Vroom
1932-	Charles S. Walton, Jr., Chairman
1957-	H. Stewart Warner
1939-	Thornley B. Wood, Assistant Secretary

OFFICERS OF THE BOARD OF TRUSTEES

CHAIRMEN

March-November	1925	Frank M. Goodchild
	1925-39	James A. Maxwell
	1939-	Charles S. Walton, Jr.

FIRST VICE CHAIRMEN

March-November	1925	James A. Maxwell
	1925-39; 1939-47	Wesley H. Hoot
	1929-39	Curtis L. Laws
	1947-	Paul E. Almquist

SECOND VICE CHAIRMEN

March-July	1925	David Lee Jamison
July-November	1925; 1927-29	Curtis L. Laws
November	1925-27	Frank Earle Parham
	1929-39	W. Theodore Taylor
	1939-48	M. Joseph Twomey

SECRETARIES

March-November	1925	Ralph L. Mayberry
November	1925-41	John A. Hainer
	1941-44	P. Vanis Slawter
	1944-	Gordon H. Baker

ASSISTANT SECRETARIES

1928-41	P. Vanis Slawter
1941-	Thornley B. Wood

TREASURERS

1925-43	Ralph I. Levering
1943	Harvey Bartle

ASSISTANT TREASURERS

1928-32; 1936-56	Joseph Hill
1932-34	R. J. Wadsworth
1934-36	Harry W. Barras

FORMER FACULTY MEMBERS

ADAMS, William W.; Professor of New Testament, 1925-46.

ANDERSON, Helen D.; Dean of Women's Activities (College Division). 1944-48.

BALL, Charles T.; President, 1925-26.

BARRAS, Harry W.; Professor of Homiletics, 1925-36.

BOWMAN, Joseph R.; Professor of Christian Music, 1936-52; Professor of Fine Arts, 1946-52; Registrar, 1945-

BROWN, L. Sarle; Director of Department of Christian Music, 1925-52; Professor of Voice, 1925-52.

CHAMPION, John B.; Professor of Christian Doctrine, 1925-41.

COOLEY, Paul B.; Assistant Professor of English Language and Literature (College Division), 1944-46.

de BLOIS, Austen K.; President, 1926-36.

ELLIOTT, Willis E.; Professor of Greek and Hebrew (College Division), 1946-49.

ELMORE, Wilber T.; Professor of Missionary and Christian History, 1925-35.

GORHAN, Donald R.; Professor and Director of School of Education, 1931-43.

GRIFFITHS, William E.; Instructor of Theology, 1930-36; Assistant Professor of Old Testatment Interpretation and Hebrew, 1937-38; Professor of Old Testament Interpretation and Hebrew, 1938-52.

HANSEN, M. Elizabeth (Williams); Director of Women's Activities (College Division), 1943-44.

HARRIS, Arthur E.; Registrar and Professor of Psychology, Secretary of Faculty and Director of Extension Division, 1925-38; Professor of Biblical Introduction, 1938-50.

JACKSON, Herbert; Professor of Missions, 1951-54.

JAMISON, David L.; Professor of Philosophy of Religion, 1925-41.

JONES, Irene A.; Dean of Women (College Division), 1934-43.

LIVINGSTON, Benjamin L.; Professor of Evangelism and Director of Field Work, 1930-41.

MASSEE, Jasper C.; Guest Professor of Homiletics, 1938-41.

MAXWELL, James A.; Professor of English Bible, 1926-48.

MUELLER, William A.; Professor of Christian History, 1936-45.

ORTEGON, Samuel M.; Professor of Spanish and Sociology (College Division), 1946-52.

PALMER, Gordon; President, 1936-48.

REIFF, Evan A.; Professor of English (College Division), 1946-50.

RODDY, Clarence S.; The James Maxwell chair of English Bible and Hermeneutics, 1944-51.

RUTENBER, Culbert G.; Professor of Philosophy of Religion and Christian Ethics, 1939-58.

SNYDER, Virginia; Instructor of Music (College Division), 1929-49; Professor of Music (College Division), 1949-54.

STILWELL, Herbert F.; Professor of Evangelism, 1926-30.

SWOPE, George W.; Professor of Evangelism, 1925-26.

TAYLOR, Barnard C.; Professor of Old Testament Interpretation, 1925-37.

TEASDALE, Ruth H.; Director of Women's Activities and Instructor of Education (College Division), 1948-

TELFORD, James H.; Professor of Missions and Allied Subjects, 1943-49.

TORBET, Robert G.; Instructor of Literature (College Division), 1934-37; Instructor of Literature and History (College Division), 1937-38; Professor of Literature and History (College Division), 1938-44; Professor of Christian History, 1944-51.

WORTLEY, George F.; Director of School of Religious Education, 1926-30.

WRIGHTON, William H.; Professor of Homiletics and Evangelism and English Bible, 1941-44.

PRESENT FACULTY MEMBERS

BAKER, Nelson B.; Professor of English Bible.

BENDER, Thorwald W.; Professor of Philosophy of Religion and Theology.

CRABTREE, Arthur B.; Professor of Theology.

DALGLISH, Edward R.; Professor of Old Testament Interpretation and Hebrew.

DAVIS, Walter B.; Professor of Missions.

GUFFIN, Gilbert L.; President; Professor of Pastoral Theology.

HAND, William J.; Associate Professor of Bibliography; Librarian.

HEATON, C. Adrian; Professor of Christian Education (President-elect, California Baptist Theological Seminary beginning his work in middle of year).

HEATON, Ada Beth; Profesor of Christian Education (resigning in course of year to join her husband in service at the California Baptist Theological Seminary).

MARING, Norman H.; Professor of Church History; Registrar.

MORGAN, Carl H.; Professor of New Testament Interpretation and Greek; Dean.

PAULLIN, Norman W.; Professor of Evangelism and Pastoral Ministry.

POWERS, William E.; Professor of Theology.

WILLIAMS, Albert G.; Professor of Homiletics.

SEMINARY LECTURERS
1925-1960

ANDERSON, Joel A. (Christian Music)
BARTLE, Harvey, Jr. (Psychiatry and Pastoral Counselling)
BLACKWOOD, Andrew W. (Homiletics)
BOWMAN, Joseph R. (Christian Music and Worship)
BYITTE, John L. (Pastoral Care)
ELMORE, Maud J. (Missions)
FREW, Allan M. (Homiletics)
KOCH, Glenn A. (Greek and Hebrew)
McGee, Theron C. (Christian Education)
MANGHAM, Walter G., Jr. (Music and Speech)
MAYE, Arthur (Christian Education)
RENNE, Frida E. (Christian Education)
SAWIN, Margaret (Christian Education)
SMITH, Ethel (Speech)
SNYDER, Virginia (Music and Speech)
TURNER, James B.
WARD, Margaret S. (Christian Education)
WORRELL, Edward K. (Christian Education)

COLLEGE DIVISION INSTRUCTORS
1925-1952

ANDERSON, Maxine (Music)
ASQUITH, Glenn H. (French and Sociology)
BARTLE, Harvey Jr. (Psychology)
BECHTEL, Leland P. (Psychology)
BROKAW, Rhena G. (Mathematics and Spanish)
BROWN, Daisy A. (Music)
BROWNE, Rachel S. (Music)
CAMPBELL, Robert (Greek and Hebrew)
CEDARHOLM, Myron B. (Psychology)
CLAGHORN, George S. (Philosophy)
DAUGMAN, John (German)
DAWSON, Esther T. (Music)
DEMAREST, Charles N. (Music)
ENNIS, Charles (Music)
FERRE, Margaret V. (German)
GIBSON, L. Tucker (Education)
HAGAR, Emily S. (Music)
GERMAN, William J. (German and Hebrew)
HESTER, James D. (Speech)
HINE, Leland D. (History)

HUGAR, Nellie B. (Music)
HUNTER, Charles E. (Sociology)
JAYNE, Marion V. (Music)
KINDLEBERGER, Mary M. (Music)
KUTNOW, Orpha (English)
LILLICK, Edna
MARKEY, George (Music)
MARTIN, James (Sociology and Christian Education)
MATTHEWS, Harry A. (Music)
MAXWELL, Helen (English)
MOODY, Boyce Hudson (History)
PENDLETON, Flordora M. (Music)
PIETI, Lauri (Music)
PINTO, Jose de Miranda (Spanish)
ROBERTSON, Gordon (Missions)
ROBINSON, Newell (Music)
RODRIQUEZ, Oscar (Spanish)
SHANE, Mae D. (Christian Education)
SIBLEY, Marguerite (Music)
STEIN, Marion L. (Music)
STURGIS, Russell D. (Biology)
SULLY, Eva F. (Music)
TAYLOR, Irene C. (Music)
THOMPSON, Catherine (Missions)
TIMMINGS, William T. (Music)
VANAMAN, Grace R. (Commercial Studies)
VAUGHN, Gordon L. (Mathematics)